AFFIRMATIONS FOR WHEN YOU LOVE AGAIN

SEFRA KOBRIN PITZELE

Health Communications, Inc.
Deerfield Beach, Florida

©1992 Sefra Kobrin Pitzele
ISBN 1-55874-211-5

Publisher: Health Communications, Inc.
          3201 S.W. 15th Street
          Deerfield Beach, FL 33442-8190

To The Reader

After writing *Surviving Divorce: Daily Affirmations*, I began to get letters reminding me how many people have gone through divorce and have gone on to marry again. Others reminded me that not all people have been married, but most have known the joy of love more than once in their lives.

In general, people want to move on to new relationships but sometimes don't know how to begin. Others are frightened that they may repeat the same behaviors which added to past discord. By far the largest group are those already in love — or at least in serious "like" — who need a sense of direction and a gentle nudge to get going again.

Affirmations For When You Love Again is a natural spin-off from writing about divorce. While some people have sworn off marriage and relationships forever, most of us look forward to our second chance — a chance to love again.

This book is dedicated, with love, to every brave person who has gone through the pain of a failed relationship or marriage, who has had the emotional strength to take a good, hard, honest look at their habits and behaviors, and who is willing to grow and create personal change in order to love again — this time in an equal, successful and contented fashion.

Just as there are certain ingredients that make the perfect chocolate cake, there is a similar need for the right ingredients to make the love between two people work.

Take two parts unselfishness and one part patience, and work together. Add plenty of industry. Lighten with good will and sweeten with kindness. Put in smiles as thick as raisins in plum pudding, and bake by the warmth which streams from a loving heart. If this fails to make you happy, the fault is not with the recipe, but with the cook.

It is now up to both cooks to continue stirring in order to be sure the end result is both good and leaves you content.

· · · · · · · · ·

We are well on our way to
"cooking up" a great marriage. Together,
with continual work, we will
bake to perfection.

What a gift a second marriage or second love can be. Knowing that another person feels about you the way you feel about them, knowing that their heart lurches each time you come into view or with every phone call, causes pure and unadulterated joy.

Moving into a "new love" with an open heart, an ability to compromise and the willingness to fight fairly and talk openly means we have some of the key ingredients to making love work.

If we have left a love or marriage that didn't work well, we can now bring to our new love all that we have learned.

. . . .

At my stage of life,
I am ready to work hard to keep
my new love growing.

She was waiting for her airplane when an announcement came over the loudspeaker. "Mr. Johnson, please come to American Airlines check-in area to reclaim your personal possessions."

Bingo! Joanne felt her stomach lurch. For years she had been in a marriage in which her husband had treated her just like a possession. Her sudden awareness of something she had known all along, but was unwilling to admit even to herself, was a relief.

She had stayed because of the children and because he made a good living. Finally, Joanne felt so damaged and used that she reclaimed herself and began a new life.

· · · · · · · ·

I own myself and can claim
all that is me, both good and bad.

We hear it over and over. Practice safe sex. Protect yourself. Even a recent segment on the program "Golden Girls" showed those intrepid ladies in a drugstore purchasing condoms.

Just as important as safe sex is our need to practice respect for ourselves. Falling in love doesn't necessarily imply that sex will follow closely on its heels, or even on its heels at all. But if it does, while it may not always be convenient, we should never lose sight of the importance of safe sex.

By taking time and letting our new relationships develop slowly, safe sex will become one petal on a newly blooming rose.

• • • • • • • •

I respect myself and can take
the time to be both safe and happy.

Jim sat in the coffee shop with a few close friends from his support group. "Nah, I'm never trying marriage again. I really got stomped on during my divorce." His friends were sympathetic and offered what Jim rarely got anywhere else — unqualified love and support. He felt emotionally safe when he was with close friends.

After two years of living alone, Jim began to long for some female companionship. He recognized what so many of us have painfully acknowledged — that this is a world built for couples where he felt constantly out of step being alone. Jim took the first step and asked a woman out, and he soon recognized how much he had missed female companionship.

· · · · · · · ·

I am ready now to begin dating
and recognize I need to take
this one step at a time.

"She said she couldn't live with me any longer, that she loved me, but it seemed impossible for her to carry on a conversation with me." Jose was very upset as he shared why his marriage had ended.

Like a turtle who pulls in his head every time his shell is tapped, Jose had been protecting himself with his emotional armor. He tried to stay as invisible as possible so he wouldn't be whipped again.

Jose wanted desperately to love again. In fact, what he wanted most was to win his wife back. So he found the kink in his armor and began to chisel away at his old defensive behavior, hoping to improve those character deficits which had frightened her away.

• • • • • • • •

As I let myself be
more vulnerable, I am beginning
to recognize I do have the right to feel
and to share my feelings.

"This time," Harvey said emphatically, "I'm going to make my marriage work!"

"What makes you think number four is going to be any different from numbers one, two or three?" his sister Tessa asked. "You just keep making the same mistakes over and over again. Aren't you ever going to learn?"

Finally realizing that what she was saying really made sense, Harvey set out on a journey of self-discovery to find out why all his marriages failed. Through a colleague at work he found an ACoA group and began to attend meetings faithfully.

"I never knew how our father's drinking played such a big role in how I act and who I am. I thought if I hid myself from his problem, I wouldn't be affected. I really want to stay in love with my current girlfriend, so I'm going to work hard to make it work."

. . . .

I am eager to change
behavior patterns I learned
in childhood.

They met in a bar, which was, unfortunately, an obvious place for two kids from heavy-drinking families to meet. After a few months they married. They were so good-looking that people commented they looked just like "Barbie" and "Ken" dolls.

Eight years and three children later, "Ken" decided to stop drinking — cold turkey — but his wife still tipped the bottle regularly. Eventually, he went to AA and then ACoA meetings as well. He grew, stretched and matured. She kept drinking and he kept trying to get her to stop.

Believing totally in the marriage vows which stated "for better or for worse," he decided to stay married and to accept her as she was, hoping some day she too would want to change.

• • • • • • • •

I can only create change in
myself, but I need not be
co-dependent either.

Back to the Future, Parts I, II and *III* have been extremely successful movies. Unfortunately, when we have a failed relationship, we may find our life going *Back to the Past, Part II.*

Without even understanding why, people who are co-dependent find themselves falling in love again and again with a person who has similar, if not identical, problems to the ones already left behind.

Being drawn into a co-dependent relationship shows we have gained little or no insight about our own weaknesses. Not until we can move away from being co-dependent — and that usually requires help from others — can we truly develop a healthy and autonomous love.

• • • • • • • •

Working on my problems is
hard work, but I know the rewards
will more than equal the pain.

Deep within every one of us there dwells a place where we hide our hurtful family secrets. Sometimes this place is so deep within our minds, we aren't really aware of the problem.

When a couple isn't able to have complete trust in one another — when family secrets stay deeply hidden — the relationship is usually doomed to fail before it has really begun.

In order to be free of our past, we may need help letting go of our secrets. Once the secrets come out of their dark box, we become more free to make grown-up decisions about love and loving.

. . . .

I am ready now to look
within my shadow place to free
my secrets.

Out to dinner with old friends, Sari was near tears. "I just don't understand it. Tom and I have so much fun together. I love him and I know he loves me; he's told me so many times. We're great together in bed; we're great when we're not in bed. But whenever I mention the "M" word, he changes the subject.

"He even talks to me about our future, our children, but he just won't talk about actually getting married. Now I'm getting out of the best relationship I've ever had in my life."

Sari's friends helped her understand that the problem was his, that some people just aren't emotionally able to commit to a lifetime relationship.

• • • • • • • •

*I won't let his fear of
commitment stop me from loving.
I am worthy and I will find
the right person to love.*

11

Carrying hidden anger for a long time or "stuffing" our feelings so we can barely identify our own emotions of warmth and caring, takes a tremendous amount of physical and emotional energy.

People abused during childhood may not even recognize how angry they really are, but their faces often show it and so do their body mechanics.

Identifying feelings of anger and their source are the first steps to letting go. Letting go of anger is necessary in order to make love work. Expressing feelings is important for maturity, and those of us who suppress anger soon recognize how difficult it is to keep holding it in.

• • • • • • • •

Anger is one letter short of
danger. I am ready, with help, to move
from this anger-filled place.

A whole series of unsuccessful relationships, one after another, leave the person who is constantly told, "It's over between us," feeling more and more emotionally damaged and fragile.

Reaching out for love in all the wrong places and in all the wrong ways is no way to begin a relationship. Having heart-to-heart talks with past loves and really being willing to hear personal criticism is very difficult and not always practical.

Being willing to work on what you perceive as the reasons for the people you loved to leave, perhaps in therapy or in a group, will begin the process of self-discovery, growth and change.

. . . .

I claim my shortcomings
and know I can convert them to
personal strengths.

"Chocolate attack!" is a scream commonly heard, especially among women, when a current lover breaks it off and ends the relationship. Needing chocolate is actually our body telling us what it needs. Chocolate produces a substance called phenylethylamine — that we produce naturally when we are on the "high" of being in love.

Two good friends, both having recently been told, "It's over," may gorge themselves on hot fudge sundaes and be equally dismayed to find relief is only temporary.

What matters is not the chocolate, but not having to suffer alone. Once we've shared sad feelings, we often find ourselves open again to meeting new people.

· · · · · · · ·

I will only feel miserable
for a short period of time. I know
from past experience that I'll
be open to a new love soon.

"She was so good," Tim started to say, when his entire bowling team turned and chorused, "How good was she?"

"Hey, you guys. This isn't The Johnny Carson Show; this is serious stuff. How could we be so terrific together sometimes and fight like pit bulls most of the rest of the time? I just don't get it."

Sometimes a relationship, if it can be called that, is purely sexual. An almost obvious animal attraction permeates the room and the two lovers are pulled together like the two poles of a magnet. But that's sex, not love.

. . . .

*Good sex is enough
once in a while, but I am ready
now for a relationship that
extends beyond the bed.*

It took nearly three years after Susan broke her engagement to start dating again. During that time she did extensive reading in the self-help area and joined a women's support group.

Seeing a therapist, digging deep to begin to find the source of her problems and working hard to be more emotionally healthy was difficult. But she kept at it.

Finally she began to feel whole again. She was finally confident in her ability to care for her emotional and physical needs, and she had learned to enjoy her own company as well.

. . . .

I am ready to fall in love
with someone who will augment,
not be, my life.

Myra was very specific when she decided
to see a therapist. "I'm willing to come and
listen, but please don't hurt me."

Many of us who begin therapy know we
need to grieve in order to move on. In
Myra's case, having come from a 20-year
verbally abusive marriage, she was realistically frightened about showing her deepest
feelings — of telling the whole truth — lest
she be open to abuse once again.

Fortunately, her therapist was sensitive to
her needs and began therapy compassionate-
ly and with respect for Myra's fears. Before
too long Myra trusted him and was able to
really open herself to begin the hard work
that treatment involves in order to grow.

· · · · · · · · ·

While I am afraid to hurt
and to be hurt, I am willing to expose
my feelings to grow.

Family Codes

Adults who grew up in dysfunctional homes where they were neither adored nor praised as children, who learned to hide away their emotions, are among the least likely to succeed at loving.

In many instances they fall in love with a person who has grown up with a similar family code of silence and behavior, and who also has not worked through their own personal problems.

It isn't until two mature adults meet and fall in love that the relationship stands a good chance of being successful. Maturity comes not from age, but from willingness to change and grow as our own needs grow.

• • • • • • • •

I left childhood in a cocoon,
but I will soon emerge
a butterfly.

It's no easy task to meet available single adults these days. Bar-hopping and other such activities are taboo, due to AIDS and other sexually-transmitted diseases. We all need to be very careful to protect ourselves.

Most of us have learned to go to "mixers" at church or temple; to take classes where we might meet interesting new people; to attend "Parents Without Partners" meetings; to join a gym or to become involved with volunteer causes. New sexual mores encourage healthier ways for singles to meet potential partners.

Rather than actively looking for someone to love, most of us have decided to pursue exciting new interests and take life day by day.

· · · · · · · ·

I will find exciting and
safe new ways to take care
of myself.

"I didn't realize how little I really knew about myself," Helene explained. "Herb always took such good care of everything — the house, the bills, the kid's tuition. And I was really happy, at least I thought I was, until he ran away with that office manager. Where did I go wrong?"

Helene, like many of us, had become hooked on being Herb's wife. She used his status and his life as a substitute for her own.

She understood now that she had a great deal to learn about her weaknesses and her dependencies. She was a stubborn woman but very determined to learn.

• • • • • • • •

I am learning to be strong,
to be my own person.

Some of us say we can forgive the past transgressions of our loved ones, but, in truth, we can't seem to completely forget. Even as we seem ready to move into a new relationship, we may still have the ghost of our past sitting squarely upon our shoulders.

Not until true forgiveness occurs can we let go. It's not always necessary to confront the errant spouse, but instead to do some hard personal work to shake off battered dreams and bitter memories.

Carrying hatred and anger takes a tremendous amount of energy. It's hard to give them up if we have held them close as part of who we are. But not until we let them go will we be free to love again.

· · · · · · · ·

I have forgiven both my
ex-spouse and myself. I am ready
now to love again.

Most of us have noticed people who actually recoil when they are touched, especially unexpectedly. It's not too hard to figure out that these folks have been touched inappropriately in their lives — sexually abused or perhaps beaten when they were younger.

Learning to accept touch is crucial for loving, since a relationship can't survive without touching, holding or hugging. Learning to handle being touched and then to welcome it may be a long and emotionally painful process.

With the help of a therapist, a sex therapist or even a masseuse, one can learn to handle being touched by another person. Hopefully touching will soon be anticipated as a wonderful part of a love relationship.

· · · · · · · ·

I want to love myself
so I can learn to love
another.

22

Most of us have heard about "the law of diminishing returns." Somehow we never expected it to become the story of our love relationships. It may seem that the more we give of ourselves, the less we have returned to us.

It's hard to understand that in a strong, healthy love relationship one should get back as much as one gives. In order to achieve balance and keep love strong, it's necessary to grow together, to make mature decisions together and to always remember to consider your loved one's feelings — often over your own.

Give and take isn't natural to some people, but like riding a bike or playing a guitar, it can be learned.

· · · · · · · ·

"Diminishing returns"
is out for me. An investment in
myself now will help me get
back as much as I give.

They had what appeared to be the ideal marriage. Yolanda and Ned were open, affectionate and spontaneous when with friends. But they shared a problem at home — in fact, it was a deep secret. Ned was gay and had married without telling Yolanda about his sexual orientation. It didn't take her long to figure it out and confront him. For a long time she stayed with him, even with no sex, because she really did love him.

But her needs mattered too, and finally they separated and divorced. Their friends didn't understand how she could leave her "perfect" husband and move almost immediately to another state and soon into another marriage.

Her feelings about Ned remained strong, and Yolanda never told his secret.

• • • • • • • •

Some secrets are meant
to be kept, for telling the truth
only hurts the ones we love.

They saw it coming as surely as a summer storm, but neither had the skills needed to stop their continual bickering. This was a couple who had both been married previously. Butting heads like bucks fighting for superiority and territory, they continually knocked each other with abusive comments covered by humor.

They did love each other and neither understood the real problem, so they risked it all, laid their feelings on the line and went together for marriage counseling.

They stuck it out, and when they loved again, it was in a new way, with respect, with caring and with one another.

· · · · · · · ·

We have learned that we
can support and accept one another
without giving up our own need
to be equal and respected.

Oh, the secrets we keep! And how often they needn't be kept secret at all. There is too much secrecy in this world, too many people frightened about their past, about their present and about their future.

Saying a secret out loud, first alone and then in front of others, often diminishes its power. "My mother used to bathe me and touch me, until I was ten," whispered Art.

"I used to masturbate every time I heard my parents making love. It really excited me," shared Joanne.

Patrice smiled shyly. "I did, too — masturbate, I mean. I actually still do." To their collective surprise no one in the group shunned them. Their friends stayed their friends. Everyone has a secret, and sometimes it's not nearly as frightening when it's out in the open.

· · · · · · · ·

Giving up a secret
gives back a piece of me I'd
kept hidden away.

All of us know couples who started dating in high school and got married shortly after. Marie and Ben were one of those couples. They were both 17 and seniors when Marie got pregnant, but it didn't bother them since they had planned to get married anyway. Ben quit school a few months short of graduation to work in the local factory, and Marie delivered twins.

For a few years life was good. Marie went to work and through her job took free college classes. Before she knew it she had earned her college degree, then a master's. Ben still worked in the factory. When Marie received a terrific job offer in a distant city, Ben refused to leave his job.

She loved him still, but finally realized he hadn't grown as she had, so she packed up the twins and moved away.

· · · · · · · ·

When only one person grows,
the growing is usually apart.

It's only at home with our loved ones or perhaps with roommates that we can strip down to our "real core." At home, as long as we don't have company, we can wear our ratty old robe all day on Sunday and even eat ice cream or drink milk out of the container. After all, this is where we live, and certain behaviors are tolerated at certain times.

When we are with loved ones, we feel safe. We know no one will criticize because we wear old robes and spread the Sunday paper out all over the living room floor.

Feeling completely safe with a person you love and are loved by is one of the best parts of being in love — first or second time around.

· · · · · · · ·

I feel accepted and loved
just as I am.

It's amazing how often we can read our loved ones' moods before they even enter the room. After all, there's a huge difference between coming home whistling and kicking the garbage can, or between a slouching, dejected look and a proud and happy strut.

Marriages fail sometimes because both people are too sensitive and try too hard to read feelings into body language. Some people aren't even aware of what messages their body posture is sending.

If this has been a sore point in a relationship, perhaps the one who is always trying to interpret behavior is really the one who needs help.

· · · · · · · ·

*I understand from my childhood
why I am oversensitive to "body talk."
I am learning to desensitize.*

No matter how good our family of origin was, each of us feels a deficit in one area or another. Some of us were "underloved" — not on purpose perhaps — we just didn't get enough unqualified love. Others were "overloved" — asked to measure up to impossible standards like getting straight A's, being captain of the football team and altar boy, as well as being the perfect "little adult."

As we matured, many of us have learned how to get what we needed as children. Those who felt "underloved" may find themselves with an expressive, expansive and inclusive mate.

So long as we don't swing too far the other way to become the opposite of who we were as children, we can keep our Inner Child and outer adult in balance.

• • • • • • • •

Keeping balance is not easy work,
but it's important for me
to persist.

Just because we may have come from a less-than-perfect family is no reason to assume we will not have strong and loving relationships as adults. Like the flame under a simmering stew, we must continually make adjustments so no one is simmering and no one is stewing.

People can and often do overcome a difficult childhood with warmth, love, understanding and considerable personal insight. It takes work, but once we are aware of the issue, most of us work on the problem.

Unhappy family patterns, contrary to popular belief, need not always be repeated. New and more comfortable patterns can be learned.

• • • • • • • •

*I love with no qualifications
and am loved in the same way. We will
continue to adjust to each other's
needs and the needs of
our family.*

For some people childhood is a miserable time of life and the family abode is not a haven. Most of us gain understanding as adults about why we act the way we do in certain situations and how we can create personal change.

"Family blood," at least from our family of origin, is not always thicker than water. Our new family, our husband or wife and children can offer the stability we never had as children, just so we work hard at staying stable.

A new love presents brand-new and wonderful opportunities. What we make of them is up to us.

. . . .

There is no rule that says
I have to love or take care of my parents.
I have chosen to not be with them,
and my decision makes me
emotionally stronger.

It's the strangest thing about intuition — when our own intuition says, "Don't," "Danger" or "You better stay away," it would be a good idea to take heed. Yet, for some reason beyond our understanding we often persist.

When our inner core is sending out vibrations of "Forget it," we should stop pursuing a person to date or have a relationship with. Something about that person or about how he or she brings up childhood memories pushes our awareness and fear buttons.

We should try to listen to our "sixth sense" — our sense of intuition. It rarely leads us astray.

• • • • • • • •

*Even though it may not be
obvious, when my inner self warns
me away from a person, I know
enough to listen.*

The best surprise of all, after a marriage or long-term love relationship breaks up, is when we discover that we have great inner strength and can rely on ourselves to fill our own needs.

Once we fully recognize our own personal worth and know that we are strong and able to take care of ourselves in or out of a long-term relationship, we can move on, knowing we can always rely on ourselves.

Being able to gain more maturity from adversity is a difficult but wonderful way to become a stronger, more independent person.

•••••••

I do not need to depend on another
person to feel whole.

One of the most delightful surprises that can happen as our children grow up is the beginning of our adult relationship with them. Many of us were not really aware our official parenting years were over until our long-term marriage broke up and we were forced to notice.

Children who are adults are often far more philosophical about the end of our marriage than we ever could be, and they can often put things in perspective for us quickly. They begin to give us advice — useful and surprisingly practical advice.

As we begin to date and perhaps fall in love, we are pleased and proud to find our adult children can be our biggest boosters.

· · · · · · · ·

I am learning anew that my adult children have become my friends.

Depending upon the type of family they were raised in, some men may feel that any woman who is friendly, warm and giving always wants something from them.

Having been raised by a mother who used all her feminine wiles for personal gain and having a wife who might have done the same, these men could easily feel threatened when they enter a relationship with a woman who is naturally warm and spontaneous.

They may either leave or send out strong messages that say, "Stay away, I don't need you." How sad for them.

· · · · · · · ·

I can learn to be more open and trusting.

There are certain warning signs that tell us we have ventured into a dangerous area when dealing with a new love. We need to be aware that not all new "steadies" are good for us.

For example, if the person you are dating is extremely controlling, you might want to think twice before committing. Trying to cut you off from your family and friends so he or she can be the exclusive "significant other" in your life may mean trouble ahead.

Having to decide who is most important is really hard. Working toward compromise is really the best solution.

• • • • • • • •

I can protect myself by keeping
alert to potential long-term problems with
the people I date seriously.

When there was a problem with a parent or other family member who was a substance abuser, childhood problems inevitably occurred. Dealing with addiction in the family became the only way of life that that child knew.

Now, as an adult who wants to fall in love again, childhood problems may try to surface to compete, in a sense, with the dating process. We have to work hard to stay adult, to act as an adult would in our new situation.

It can be awfully hard to remind ourselves of all we have learned as adults, yet we must in order to move forward into a new and loving relationship.

. . . .

I am worthy and lovable,
and I will find the right
person to love.

Remember when we were young and wanted to earn money so badly that we would clean out the attic or garage for 50¢? When we finally got our first real job and began to feel independent, it was great. But there is another kind of earning, one that isn't so healthy.

Too often we put out extra effort to earn love, affection or respect from the people who matter most to us, just as we tried to do with our parents. We may not realize that in a balanced relationship this shouldn't be happening.

We should get back what we give, and what we give should be from love, not from what someone else owes us.

· · · · · · · ·

Worthy of love as a child,
I am also worthy as an adult.
I can give love and get love
without compromising myself.

Those famous last words, "I'm sorry it didn't work, but let's stay friends, okay?" never seem to work. We would really like to maintain a friendship with a person we once loved, but it's virtually impossible. It does work the other way, however. Often two people who were close friends go on to fall deeply in love.

Most people don't realize the value of friendship in a long-term love relationship. When the love is new, it fairly sizzles with excitement. But when love calms down, it will last if the two are best friends.

Marriage is chemistry, it's love and — most importantly — it should represent friendship for life.

• • • • • • • •

The joy of being best friends
with the one I love supports me every day.

Finally, the invitation we had been waiting for — a date to the post-game football party at the home of one of our schoolmates. We can remember even now how the sun rose and set upon being popular, feeling wanted, being in the "in" group.

Most of us can chuckle now at how important feeling popular was during high school. Experience has taught that we have the right to make our own plans and that others are often uncertain, too, even as adults.

As the company arrives, our close friends, we still marvel that they are all friends who care about us and whom we care about deeply. Married or not, in or out of a relationship, these people will always matter to us and remain friends.

. . . .

I am delighted to realize how secure
I continue to feel about
myself as an adult.

The very word *shame* carries with it the connotation of being bad. Remember the childhood chant, "Shame, shame, everybody knows your name!" Either we had done something we felt ashamed about, or the bigger or older kids said it to make us cry.

No one has the right to shame another person, yet it happens so often that millions of adults still carry the stigma of feeling they must have done something very wrong.

Still feeling shamed as an adult indicates that some serious self-work needs to be done before entering into a new love.

• • • • • • • •

Rather than repeating old behaviors,
I will see a therapist so I can always
feel proud of myself and of my
ability to share love.

Aretha really thought she had found the person with whom she would spend the rest of her life. He was perfect, a real gentleman, handsome, a smooth dancer and wonderful with all her friends and family. Everyone was crazy about Dom.

It really came as a surprise when Dom dumped her with no warning at all. Aretha was dumbfounded at first, then in a state of shock. She couldn't figure out what she had done wrong — why he didn't want her anymore.

As she struggled to regain her emotional equilibrium, Aretha recognized that she was still a strong person who could move on and live her life with or without Dom.

. . . .

I recognize now that how
other people behave sometimes
has no apparent rhyme or reason,
and that someone's leaving
was not my fault at all.

Abbey was seeing a therapist again. This time her main concern was that, even though she was in a very happy second marriage, she fantasized once in a while about the boy she had been in love with when she was fifteen. She wanted to stay married; her husband was a terrific guy.

"I even think about him and pretend it's him when Bard and I are making love — not all the time, but once in a while." Abbey was surprised when the therapist told her that many people, at one time or another, think of fantasy lovers during sex, and that as long as it was fantasy she wasn't being disloyal to her husband.

Many of us have fantasy lovers. They can add both excitement and variety to love-making.

· · · · · · · ·

I understand that having an occasional
fantasy lover may actually
enhance my marriage.

With the percentage of people getting divorced and then remarried these days, blended families and children remain one of the "top ten" areas of conversation in most new relationships. If the issue is never discussed, one usually assumes the status quo is acceptable.

With the wedding plans made and invitations mailed, your fiance suddenly informs you there will be no marriage unless your children — your beloved children — go to their other parent to live.

This is not a decision anyone should be forced to make, and it is most unfair to be given an ultimatum at the last minute. We need to think twice before we accept any ultimatum — especially one which affects not only us but our children.

· · · · · · · ·

No matter how much I am in love,
my children come first. I will
not abandon them to satisfy
my own needs.

The hurt a person feels when their love has ended, when their best friend is no more, is like nothing else we can experience. Curt was out bowling with his Tuesday night league when a beautiful woman walked by.

"You know," he told his buddies, "sometimes a guy needs to have a short fling, especially if he has been hurt like I was and needs to feel okay about himself again. It worked for me."

Charlie was appalled, but Griff laughed, "I know just what you mean, guy."

"What an archaic man you are," remarked Charlie dourly, but Curt chuckled, "Not archaic, just needy!"

"Well," his friend intoned, "remember to keep it safe."

. . . .

*Having dealt with my insecurity
around the opposite sex,
I can now move on to look for
my real, true new love.*

"I didn't realize how many women feel incomplete without a husband," remarked Sally as she and Penny were on their daily jog. "I thought I was unique for being so completely dependent on David, but I guess I'm wrong."

In fact, far too many men and women think they need a mate to complete their selfhood, to make them whole. A mature adult has a fulfilled and meaningful life with or without a long-term love.

Mature love makes life better, but doesn't, in and of itself, complete an incomplete person.

· · · · · · · ·

Life shared with the one I love is
wonderful, but if it ever ends,
I shall still be a strong, independent
and fulfilled person.

"I didn't know he was abusing me. I just didn't know. I mean, I knew something wasn't right with the way he always threw temper tantrums, but he never tried to hit me or anything," Trudi shared at bridge club one afternoon. "I feel so stupid for letting it go on all these years."

While emotional abuse doesn't often send one to the emergency room, it should well send a person to seek a psychiatrist's care. Damaged self-esteem is very hard to repair. So are damaged hearts.

No one needs to live with another human being who threatens violence, intimidates through body language or threatens to destroy your property.

• • • • • • • •

I have enough strength and emotional support
to leave this unhealthy marriage.

Remember your feelings the first time you were seriously in love? While it may not have happened at first sight, before too much time passed you knew this was the one, the right love for you, your one and only for life.

Now you find yourself single again, sometimes with a great sense of relief, other times with deep sorrow — but alone all the same. Most of us want to feel comfortable about ourselves. In order to be peaceful and content, it's likely we will have to do some self-work. We've been part of a twosome and now we are alone. It takes hard and painful work to grow.

Groups and therapy may be necessary to help us identify our hurt feelings and to begin healing. The road may be bumpy, but the trip is worth the trouble.

· · · · · · · ·

I am willing to work on my personal problems
in order to move forward in my life.

Hope, as they always say, springs eternal. When a person we have dearly loved has left us — sometimes with reason, sometimes for no apparent reason — many of us may become lost for a while in our grief.

Yet the human spirit always tries to bounce back. Hoping to meet someone new isn't enough. We must put forth the effort to go out, to be social and to put ourselves in places — like interesting classes, for example — to meet new friends.

Hope alone isn't enough, but it does serve as a wonderful starting point.

• • • • • • • •

I know the first effort has to be mine,
but even as I leave my house,
I will continue to hope I'll
meet someone special.

"You are so stubborn!" This is a refrain many of us have heard from time to time in our lives. If we were in an unhealthy relationship, we may have heard other unkind phrases as well.

When we are ready to love again, it is time to evaluate our strengths and weaknesses. If being too stubborn is a character defect, then learning to compromise is one goal we can set our sights on achieving.

The gentle art of knowing how to compromise, without giving up too much of ourselves, leaves everyone in a win-win situation.

. . . .

*I am willing to work on my ability
to compromise, but I will not
compromise my personal ideals.*

For a long while after the marriage or love affair is over, we may still feel hurt and abandoned. Spending long periods wondering what was wrong with us, why our loved one "bailed out," helps pass the time but doesn't provide grounds for fertile new growth.

Every experience in our lives causes us to change. We are obviously different now than when we were younger, and we are never the same after children as before.

Taking the change that naturally occurs from loss of a love and turning it into positive growth shows maturity and readiness for new experiences.

· · · · · · · ·

As I accept the change that occurs
in my life, I understand
I am finally becoming a mature adult.

Ah! That green-eyed monster rears its ugly head. Even when we knew the love was over, even if we wanted it to be over, the very first time we bump into our "ex" (husband, wife, lover), our heart may do an unexpected and thoroughly perplexing thump. We suddenly remember how comfortable, warm and toasty it felt when we were once holding hands in the same intimate way he or she is holding hands with someone else now.

What we are jealous of, what we finally recognize, is that the "ex" has someone new to love and we do not — yet. It even can feel mildly embarrassing when that oft-dreaded first accidental meeting happens.

· · · · · · · · ·

I miss being married. I know I do not miss who I was married to.

Rafe felt self-conscious at his cousin's baptism. Everywhere he looked was another family member, happily married and with a flock of children. He was tired of being alone.

An all-too-common trap we fall into is wanting to be married just for the sake of having a mate. What matters most is that we first become independent, autonomous people on our own.

Then when we look for the right person to love, they do not become our whole life, but a delightful add-on to an already good lifestyle.

· · · · · · · ·

Like winning the lottery, the joy of
finding the right person
to love is a bonus to my already
worthwhile life.

At home Marley was a wonderful wife and mother. She was the envy of everyone in the neighborhood with her trim figure, well-behaved children and full-time job. She and Don had a good solid marriage.

Out in public was another story altogether. When Marley had even one drink she turned, in the blink of an eye, into an abusive, name-calling shrew. People who knew her from PTA were stunned to see her raking poor Don over the coals. It happened often, and Don didn't know what to do about her problem anymore.

. . . .

I am enabling my partner's abusiveness
when I stay if she or he is drinking.
I can protect my integrity and sanity by
removing myself from the scene.

It had been a provocative radio show. The topic had been, "What would you like written on your tombstone if you could say anything you want?"

Sheila was listening on the way to work and was so fascinated that she found herself musing over the topic all day. She didn't know what she would want written on hers. That evening at dinner she told Greg about the show. "What would you write, honey?" she asked.

"That's easy," he said, without missing a beat. "I'd say, 'I loved Sheila, and was blessed with the purest kind of love a man can have.' "

. . . .

*I am so grateful that our love continues
to grow each day.*

February 26 *From Love To Friendship*

They both realized it was over at the same time. Quietly Bill and Tina sat and talked. Their first two years of being in love were wonderful, but when it actually came to setting the date, neither was ready to make the commitment.

"I don't understand this," commented Bill quietly. "Let's at least stay good friends. We had too much going to give it up completely." His intentions were honorable and they really did mean to stay close, but those who have been there know that platonic friendship after true love just doesn't work.

· · · · · · · ·

*I need to figure out what was wrong
this time before I can
work on making it right next time.*

For many of us moving out of our parents' home for the first time was both frightening and exciting. We were finally old enough to be out in the world on our own. Pride continued to swell as we got a job and learned to grocery shop, cook and even balance our own personal checkbook.

The sense of being self-reliant is a wonderful empowering feeling, and one we all should feel entitled to owning. Self-reliance is a gift we bring to any long-term relationship, for part of the commitment of loving is the commitment we have to continue loving and respecting ourselves.

· · · · · · · ·

We all bring gifts to love.
Loving and respecting myself and my
abilities is one of my gifts.

We carry along with us, into every relationship, our old baggage from our past. If one of the things we are lugging around is anger at how we were raised or at a person we used to love, that anger will somehow find its way into the new relationship.

For our own sake and for the sake of the ones we love, we need to look seriously at making peace with our past, from our childhood all the way through adulthood.

Anger takes up so much energy which we can better apply toward the joy of being in love.

• • • • • • • •

*It's time now to let myself heal
from old bruises. With help
I know I can succeed.*

One of the first things he noticed after they began dating was her uncanny knack for expressing appreciation without being effusive. Somehow she made him feel like a king.

It was a great lesson to learn, and before too long he had picked up her knack of showing appreciation. By remembering to praise and thank each other, they built their love on mutual support, caring and love.

Not surprisingly, their ability to appreciate carried over at work, when they were with neighbors and especially when they had their children. By continuing to love, respect and appreciate one another, their love never dimmed.

· · · · · · · ·

Expressing appreciation — not taking
my loved one for granted — is one
way to help insure our
commitment and happiness.

Many times during the course of our lives we will find ourselves alone. This may occur if we are unmarried — by circumstance or by design — if we are between relationships or if we have simply chosen not to be involved.

There are two secrets to feeling comfortable with being alone. The first is to like ourself, to feel completely content with what and who we are and with how we live our life.

The second is to be surrounded with those who love and respect us when we feel the need for company. From our children to other family members to close friends and colleagues, who we choose to surround us is a measure of how secure we feel about ourselves.

· · · · · · · ·

Choosing to be alone
does not mean I am lonely.
Free choice gives me power to choose.

Looking for joy in all the right places sounds trite, but it is probably one of the most important traits shared by people who are happy with life.

Those of us who have learned to take negative situations and turn them upside-down to find the positive aspects, who have discovered the art of creating joyful experiences from even the most mundane days and common experiences, are truly the lucky ones.

Joy is always there. Joy is always waiting. We just have to be open to look for it in unexpected places.

· · · · · · · ·

One way for me to measure
a successful day is whether it was
filled with joy.

As she watched a couple walking through the park, Molly felt a sudden stab of jealousy. She wanted so badly to be in love again. Molly remembered vividly the feeling of being in love, of holding hands with someone special.

In fact, Molly was still tied into her feelings for her ex-husband. Two years had gone by, but she had not yet really fallen out of love. Rather than moving on to new experiences, Molly was stuck like a broken phonograph needle.

Not until we give up our old feelings, once and for all, and admit the love is truly over can we realistically look forward to holding hands once again.

• • • • • • • •

I need to look inward,
into my deep recesses of strength,
and finally give up my old feelings.

After his divorce Mike moved away and got a new job. He wasn't drinking anymore, so his job performance finally was good and he was soon promoted to foreman.

Mike, like many of us, felt proud as he created a new life for himself. One evening, in an unexpected conversation with a woman from work whom he had taken out to dinner, she asked, "Do you still miss your wife?" Taken aback, Mike really had to think about his answer.

"Just a little," he replied. "It was really hard at first, but somehow I've done okay. But yes, I do miss the good parts of our life together, just a little bit."

· · · · · · · ·

I can be honest about my past love,
my past life, without
feeling emotionally devastated.

For a long time after our love affair has ended, we may be closed up emotionally and be unreachable, even to ourselves. This can happen whether we were married or not.

Being unreachable emotionally is the way some people manage their hurt and disappointment at ending their love. Feelings of rejection and incompletion can crowd in at this time. Being aware that this can happen helps. Working hard to stay available, especially to our own needs, is most important at this time in our lives.

· · · · · · · ·

Like the clouds hiding the moon,
I shall slowly uncover my deepest feelings,
and then I will be ready to reach
out to make new friends.

We all know how to dance the courtship dance. We can't help remembering it from when we were teenagers. We meet — perhaps at a party or through a friend — and begin to look forward to phone calls and dating again.

The knowledge that something is wrong creeps up on us. The person seems friendly and warm, yet when we try to get closer, both physically and emotionally, they become inaccessible. Being inaccessible is different from being unavailable. The second we can more easily understand. Emotional inaccessibility is more difficult, especially if we have never encountered it before.

Somehow we intuitively know that this relationship has gone as far as it will go. This person is not ready to make any kind of commitment.

· · · · · · · ·

How pleased I am when I can recognize
a potential problem before it becomes full-blown and
not feel that I have failed at anything.

Sometimes we feel very needy, especially in the emotional arena. The problem comes when we know we need something — perhaps simply to be hugged, perhaps to fall in love, maybe to find a close friend — but we have no idea how to get our needs met.

It's obvious we have a need that is not being filled. What's keeping us from getting what we need? In order to find the answer to this difficult question, we may have to begin digging deeper into our lives than we were previously willing to do.

It's hard work uncovering the reasons for our unfulfilled needs, but if it's important to us to get them met, we have to undergo the risk inherent in personal growth.

• • • • • • • •

My needs are real and important to me,
and I will work hard to regain my
right to ask to have them met.

Looking forward to loving again is very exciting for most of us. Once we are over our lost love, we can readily move on to a new and wonderful experience.

If we find personal stumbling blocks in our way, it is a good idea to look both backward and forward to determine the course of our life. We might ask what in our past has caused us to carry over to a new relationship behaviors we'd rather not be bringing along.

By looking at both our past and how we imagine our future to be, we can work toward new personal goals. We can set goals of compromise, goals of showing warmth and saying "I love you," and most importantly, goals which will direct us to the path of happiness.

. . . .

I am emotionally strong enough
so I can learn to bend toward a warm
and nurturing relationship.

All that we bring to the singles world of dating has been with us ever since we were children. Our body image — how we feel about ourselves — has been deeply ingrained since we were young.

If we were lucky enough to have parents who praised us for what we could do and didn't chastise us for our failures, we likely came out of childhood feeling good about ourselves. The opposite, of course, is true as well.

Developing our body image, whether healthy or unhealthy, began when we were small children and has carried through now that we are adults. Changes we hope to make in our self-image generally need the help of a therapist, but old ideas and images can be altered.

· · · · · · · ·

*I can't be part of a
successful twosome until I work on
my feelings about myself.*

It's interesting that some people who came from families where alcohol or drug use was a matter of fact can rise above their family background and become successful, happy and loving adults, while others use their childhood as their lifetime "cause."

Rather than putting the problem in perspective, dealing with it as well as possible through one of the 12-step groups or with a private therapist, their parents' problems with addiction turn into an excuse for not doing, for not being, for not, not, not — all their lives.

Healing the problems caused by a parent's addiction becomes an irrefutable way of life, and the person can get as hooked on the cure as their parent was on substance abuse.

· · · · · · · ·

Using my childhood problems as an excuse
to not really live my life serves no one.
I want a good life and am willing to
work hard to move beyond the
problems of my parents.

Finally we have fallen in love. This time we feel certain we have chosen the right person to share our lives with, and amazingly, that person wants to share as well.

Actually, some of us may suddenly feel frightened that our new love will fail as our past love did. We enter our new love with joy, yet with a large dose of trepidation, too.

With mutual commitment, open communication and a great deal of caring, we can transform our life-long fears into a love relationship that is both safe and supportive.

. . . .

How lucky I am today!
Finally I am feeling safe, strong and
emotionally supported and supportive.

If we think back, most of us remember the exact moment when we realized it was over, that we have fallen out of love. We also remember knowing that we couldn't recapture that same love again, no matter what.

We've all been through the first true love stage; most of us remember thinking there would never be another — yet somehow there always was. In youth that moment happens much faster, much stronger and often much louder.

When we are older, falling out of love may leave us with a quiet feeling of desperation and perhaps even a willingness to compromise on those qualities and values which we know will not be good for us.

· · · · · · · ·

Even though I am frightened of
spending my mature years alone, there are
certain values and needs I will not
compromise just to have a mate.

Each of us has an ideal mate in mind. We deify them in our daydreams, only to find out that no one person can measure up to our impossible standards.

It then becomes time to look at the truth, at what we really need when we are in love. Not surprisingly, we make little compromises with ourselves. Maybe he or she is not a movie star, we think, but still good-looking. Maybe not so immaculate working around the house, but a warm and caring person.

We settle, not from desperation, but from a true understanding that we are not marrying just the wrapping — we fell in love with the whole package. Settling for a good enough marriage with fewer bells and whistles allows us to find the person to whom we are really best suited.

• • • • • • • •

A good enough marriage, one that will stand the test of time, of trials and of life's tribulations is just what I want.

It's such a common refrain that we hear it constantly. "We stayed together for the sake of our children." If we were really to take some time and give the issue some serious thought, would our children be better or worse off if we divorced? And what about ourselves?

This crucial issue should be given careful consideration, as it is deeply emotional to those of us caught in the web of a difficult marriage. After some thought, we understand that getting our personal needs met matters, too. With the problem put in these simple terms, many of us would choose to leave our marriage.

· · · · · · · · ·

Since I really wouldn't want my children to grow up in a war zone, I need not stay in one, either.

Every one of us has different physical needs and desires, and everyone of us has carried misconceptions about love and sex into our relationships.

What is a normal sex pattern? In fact, there is no such thing as "normal" for sex patterns. What matters is what each individual couple wants and communicates about. Normal for someone else may not be normal for us.

Some couples are "once-a-weekers" while others are "once a day" folks. Some dislike sex and have it rarely, if ever, while others hardly stop for food and water.

This somewhat delicate issue often needs compromise and always needs open communication. What matters is that the two people who love each other agree mutually on what is normal for them.

. . . .

No one else but my loved one
needs to know or even has a right to ask
about our marital sex patterns.

75

My, how we laughed at our parents' boring lifestyle when we were in our teen
years. "How can they be happy being with
each other all the time? Bridge on Monday,
bowling on Wednesday. How do they stand
such a boring life?" we'd wonder.

Surprisingly, the very behaviors we
laughed at as children may be exactly what
we desire most as settled adults. Most
adults like constancy in their lives just as
surely as a small child who expects a warm
dinner and a bedtime story.

After the honeymoon stage, we find that
one thing we need the most is a sense of
continuity, of constancy. In fact, as we grow
a bit older, married or not, we try to keep
our lives moving to a comfortable rhythm.

· · · · · · · ·

I am continually surprised at how
well my parents knew each other and how they
each honored the other's needs.

One would think that going for love a second time around would be easier than our first go at it. Hopefully by now we know our shortcomings, what kind of person complements our personality best and where we are headed in life.

Surprisingly, mid-life second marriages are often much harder because each partner is accompanied by the specter of their adult children and perhaps even grandchildren. We also have personal possessions which have taken years to collect and are important to us. When we were younger, we were far less encumbered.

It takes a while to feel comfortable with all the baggage, both physical and emotional, our new love brings along. Continual awareness at making a go of the relationship almost always pays off.

• • • • • • • •

A new husband or a new wife offers me a wonderful chance at a new life.

Food addiction and other food-related problems such as overeating, undereating (anorexia) or bulimia, particularly in young women, are often caused by an intense need to hide a secret. People who are addicted to food rarely do well in a long-term relationship.

Many childhood problems can cause food addiction, such as an inability to say no to others, a sense of being over-controlled most of the time or an intense need to be the "perfect" daughter, wife, mother or friend.

Fear of too much intimacy or a self-imposed feeling of emptiness often prevail. No amount of dieting or exercising will work until the original cause is uncovered and cured. Then and only then can the individual begin to deal with food issues.

· · · · · · · ·

Frightened by what I might discover,
I stayed away from therapy for years. I am so proud
that I have taken this huge first step.

Every adult needs to have close friends. For most of us the most important friend of all is the person to whom we have made a commitment for life — our husband or wife.

In order to be successful at long-term love, it is tantamount that our spouse also be our best friend. If we are lucky enough to be married to our best friend, he or she talks to us, not at us. We each allow the other "alone time" and respect each other's individual needs.

"Best friends for life" takes on a new and very important connotation as we recognize the importance of full-time sharing to our mutual well-being.

• • • • • • • •

I have cast aside my childhood
image of "best friend" as an adult and
am more than willing to share a
friend for my whole life.

How sad it is that some people have such a deep-seated need to always be right, to always prove themselves "better than." When love ends and a long relationship is over, it's not an uncommon scenario for that person to spew forth all the hurt which has been caused over the years.

Some people actually collect grievances which they have construed as personal insults and store them for future ammunition. Continually spewing pent-up old anger serves no purpose at all.

If we can open our minds instead, we may discover a potentially wonderful life. It helps when we learn to look for even the small amount of sunshine in an otherwise cloudy day. People who shed grievances like a snake sheds old skin are the ones we all want to have for our friends.

. . . .

*Instead of collecting grievances to be
used later against someone else, I will work hard
each day at collecting bits of joy to "savor."*

There are two groups of people coming forth these days on the issue of incest: those who know they were molested and those who think they might have been. Recent books released about incest say if you think you were, then you must have faith in yourself — believe it is true.

Incest victims can heal with help. They need not carry a burden all their lives which can lead to frigidity or promiscuity. Admitting or finally recognizing there is a problem, that there was molestation during childhood, and believing in oneself will help.

Seeking counseling and working through the problem may hurt, but will usually help heal the damaged child within. Also, developing friendships with people who accept you without qualification is a big step toward accepting yourself.

· · · · · · · ·

I believe in myself and my
knowledge that I was harmed as a child.
I am ready to reach out for help.

We all know at least one person who is just plain selfish. A "me-first" attitude does not play well in a long-term relationship, and we would do well to steer clear of a date, lover or potential spouse who demonstrates this childish behavior.

At times we all have the right to express a me-first attitude — when we have the flu, for example, or when someone we love is ill or dying. We often need comforting with hot soup and hugs. And we are entitled.

As we begin to date, as we recognize we are ready to get serious about a permanent romantic relationship, it would be wise to stay away from the me-first type of person.

· · · · · · · ·

*"Me-first" is the attitude I need
to adopt temporarily as I date once
again. I will look after my own
emotional needs.*

For various reasons, from dealing with a parent who was alcoholic or ill with other chronic illness to living in a single-parent family, some of us were forced by circumstances to act in an adult capacity. From cooking to cleaning to sitting, we did it all.

If a person acted as an adult when all the others around him were children, then it often happens that the same person behaves as a child when he or she should now be an adult. This is to be expected in many circumstances, and the problem needs to be worked through with professional assistance.

We need to be aware of this "turnabout" in the lives of some people so we don't inadvertently get hooked on either their personal tribulations or our need to parent the Adult Child.

• • • • • • • •

Aware now of potential problems,
I will be careful that the only children
I parent are my own.

Each one of us was raised in a different kind of home. What was normal to one might seem highly abnormal to another. For example, a person raised with a parent who had a hair-trigger temper was used to it and usually learned to stay away from the fracas.

Because of our individual family differences, we bring to each new relationship all the experiences that formed us as children. This is why some people accept the same type of behavior — in fact, expect it as their lot in life. Conversely, there are those who come from a relatively stable family with consistent discipline who look for very level people to become involved with romantically.

In order to find the right date or mate, we should first feel certain of what our personal boundaries are and not compromise them just to be involved or married.

· · · · · · · ·

I would be better off staying unmarried
than to live with someone who compromises
how I feel about myself.

It's never too late to change. It's never too late to renew oneself spiritually or move toward new personal goals. Dour people can make up their minds to be kinder and try hard to be happier. Once aware of a personal shortcoming, those who want to change their behavior badly enough can do so.

This problem presents most often when one person thinks they can change another's behavior. This never works. Never. The only way to avoid this situation is to stop dating people who make us feel uncomfortable.

While we may not understand the issue yet, we must trust our own intuition. Change and renewal can always begin if we really wish to start.

· · · · · · · ·

*I can avoid personal hurt and even
failure in a relationship by never getting
involved in the first place with
a person who has major character faults.*

Many of us remember our mother's gentle admonishment, "Go to the party, you may find someone you like." And it's true, many of us did find the right person by going somewhere we never wanted to go.

The opposite problem, when we are dating a perfectly nice person who just doesn't "ring our bell," brings another bit of mother's wisdom. "Give it time, some people grow on you." And this too is true.

Often the very best, deepest and most committed relationships came from a friendship or from a date we let "grow on us." Lucky is the person who had a mother to prod, admonish and ply us with love and good advice.

• • • • • • • •

I am grateful that I listened to
the advice to give this wonderful
person a second chance.

If our needs didn't get met as children we look for a loved one to give us what we didn't get then. From unqualified love and hugging to an enhanced sense of self-esteem, we often choose our friends on the basis of what we can give to each other.

This mutual give and take is one of the keys to successful love and marriage. Being aware of our own needs and mutually meeting each other's keeps the balance in many a marriage.

This system works well if it's only part of what happens in a marriage, and if one person is not more emotionally needy than the other. Keeping communication lines always open and non-threatening shows a couple's strength.

· · · · · · · ·

*True love means knowing what my
loved one needs and giving without being
asked, as well as getting what I
need without asking.*

There probably isn't one of us it hasn't happened to at one time or another. A very dear friend falls in love and seems to completely forget that we were ever best friends.

Forsaking all friends for a lover or spouse is usually a sign of trouble on the horizon. While the marriage is in a honeymoon period, some of this negligence is normal. If it goes on past a few months, then the new spouse might be threatened by past close friendships.

No one has the right to dictate who our friends should be. If this is happening, it may be a symptom of deeper problems.

· · · · · · · ·

There is the "we" in marriage and
the "me" in marriage. I need to remember
to keep the "me" part too, and to value
and cherish old friends.

Many of us who are parents remember our children taking our faces between their small hands and saying, "Look at me when I talk to you!"

Their plaintive cry reflects a large part of what is wrong with today's relationships — we either don't give full attention to the person who is speaking or interrupt because we are certain we know what they are going to say.

Reflective listening is the art of mirroring phrases to be sure we really understand what we are being told, using body language that shows interest and not interrupting because we are sure we "got it." Using reflective listening will help keep love strong.

• • • • • • • •

I will never be too busy or involved with my needs to listen to the one I love.

"Forget it!" Ashley said. "You'll never get me to go on a blind date." Needless to say, her friend talked her into it just one more time.

"You never know. You just might meet Mr. Right."

So Ashley accepted the date with Peter, but with serious apprehension. She had never had a decent blind date, so she didn't expect this one to work either. Her first surprise came when she opened the door to discover a tall, handsome man nearly buried in fresh roses. He smiled, handed her the roses, and said, "Wow! I almost didn't agree to this date. I can see I would have made a mistake."

Arm in arm they left, neither knowing what the future would bring, or whether they would click, but both willing to spend a pleasant evening together beginning to find out.

· · · · · · · ·

If I don't take chances, I will never be surprised.

They had been married for 36 wonderful years. When his wife suddenly died, Cole missed Tina terribly. He had liked being married, having someone to go places with, to talk to, to share his life. He wanted eventually to get married again.

Recognizing that life is short and far too precious to spend alone, he set out to find the right woman to share his life. There were multitudes of widows and divorcees eager to date him, but Cole stayed the course until he found Ruth, a gentle, kind and easygoing woman who was as lonely as he.

After a six-month courtship they were sure about their love and got married, ready to move into their new marriage and into a new phase of their lives.

· · · · · · · ·

Marrying again is a wonderful tribute to the happiness I shared all those years with my first spouse.

When we are young parents and in love, it seems only normal for us to work hard. After all, most of us want a nice home and to raise happy, healthy children.

A problem can arise with men whose fathers were often absent when they were children. These men may become absent in the same way. Perhaps the father works long hard hours and feels justified in "taking a break" away from his family. Maybe he feels unsure how to be a strong parent. This is sad, as it leaves all the parenting to the mother.

Whatever the reason, men whose fathers were absent may also become absent parents themselves. Unless it is pointed out and they seek counseling, it is entirely possible their sons may become absent fathers, too.

. . . .

I was angry that my father was always gone.
I will be a stronger parent than he,
but I see I'm going to need
some help to learn how.

"No way! You never told me you had children. I don't like kids. Forget it!" What a message to get from a person we were just becoming attached to — that rare type of person who seemed to have some potential to fit into our future.

Of course, it was our fault to begin with. Our children are our responsibility and should never be denied or hidden. They should always be part of the package. "Love me, love my kids."

Certainly children may present a problem when we are dating again, but denying we have them not only devalues the children, it also devalues us. While it may not always be fun to have children, we do have them and they are, indeed, part of the package.

• • • • • • • •

My children are my responsibility and shirking it only tends to diminish both mine and other people's opinion of me. I accept my responsibility willingly.

It can be so exciting and so wonderful when we finally connect with a person and feel the genuine possibility of commitment. There is bounce to our step, anticipation for each new day and eagerness for the next time we can be together.

Some of us let our physical needs rule our body and confuse lovemaking with love. When we do fall in love, we need it to be with the "whole package" — the whole person. Especially these days, we need to be careful about jumping the gun before we know if what we are feeling is mutual and permanent.

True maturity means holding off on purely physical needs until we know if we can satisfy each other's emotional and intellectual needs as well.

• • • • • • • •

Love does not happen in minutes but sex can.
I can put aside my physical needs and wait
until I am certain we are truly
committed to each other.

How does a person begin to date again? Many of us are scared in the beginning to even try, especially if we have been badly hurt. Starting over is a difficult problem which faces most of us when we are no longer part of a couple.

One way to begin, which at least guarantees meeting new people, is to reach out into the community by taking classes, attending an "Adjustment to Being Single" class or asking a person we know casually to go out for coffee or to a movie.

We may be surprised at how many other lonely single people there are, just waiting for an opportunity to make one or more new friends.

. . . .

My first impulse is to "hole up" so I won't risk being hurt again. I think more of myself than that and am ready to meet someone new.

Gentle words of love do not flow automatically or easily from everyone's lips. If we were raised hearing our parents say, "I love you," and they were happy with each other, we generally have a need to hear those wonderful words from the one we love.

Women and men both must learn that showing is sometimes better than telling. We should be open to read silent love messages without always hearing the actual words. Love can be shown in other ways, like being served breakfast in bed, driving the car pool without being asked or stopping at the florist on the way home for fresh flowers.

Giving and getting love messages is equally as important to men as to women. The person who shows love and the one who receives it are lucky people.

• • • • • • • •

It only takes a few moments for me to show
my love, and I will try harder to
say, "I love you," as well.

Everyone knows it takes two people to make a marriage or a commitment to a life-long love. Two to be together. Two to promise they will have a lasting relationship. Two to repeat, "in sickness and health." It takes two to make a lifelong relationship.

When the love goes wrong but one person is convinced it can be saved, then it only takes one very determined person to work at saving their love. From marriage counseling to sex therapy to a program for addiction, if the love is strong and salvageable, one person can often go all out to save it.

If the "savior" is not co-dependent, it is entirely possible that their problems can be solved, their love can be saved and they can stay together for many years to come.

. . . .

Just because a boulder has been thrown into the path of our love does not mean we have to drive off course. Even large boulders can be moved.

Very few people like to be criticized. We most likely remember incidents from childhood which hurt our feelings and demeaned us. "Sit up in that chair the way your brother and sister do!" "You did a rotten job cleaning your room. Go do it again." "You'll never amount to a hill of beans if you don't learn to do what you are told!"

As adults, when we are faced with constructive criticism from a boss or even from the one we love, the child in us still bristles. We just don't know yet how to handle ourselves. Soon we learn that criticism given gently can help us grow.

Constructive criticism can be helpful, but even good criticism needs to be given at the right moment. Offering it at the right time, when the person is receptive and not fatigued or out of sorts, usually works best.

• • • • • • • •

Constructive criticism and my willingness to
listen and act upon it have helped me.
I am proud of myself and what I can do.

Over the years we have heard the phrase, "It is better to have loved and lost than never to have loved at all." We wonder if those words are really true, since losing a love — whether it's through a break-off, a divorce or losing a spouse to death — hurts so very much.

Recent studies show that those who have been married before, even if they are separated, divorced or widowed, live longer than those who were never married (or committed to a long relationship) at all. Further, with men, particularly, getting involved and married again actually increases their lifespan.

It is easier for men to meet women than the other way around, and men tend to remarry more quickly than women do.

· · · · · · · ·

Not sharing my life with someone I love would
not be fulfilling enough for me. Part of my
happiness has been caused by my
ability to share my life and my love.

As two people grow closer together and begin to think about the permanency of their relationship, there are many things to consider. Can we live together through good and bad times? Can each of us handle the other's personal habits? What about how each will look with "grubby" clothes on — not cleaned up but the way we really are . . .

A couple has to be truly committed to each other to maintain lifelong love and sharing. Subtle problems and questions may arise which cause us to question ourselves and our commitment to one another. Total intimacy without complete honesty and sharing is not really true and lasting love.

If we are honest with each other without being hurtful, and if we totally accept the one we love, we can grow closer and eventually experience a true state of bliss.

. . . .

While not every moment of our relationship is blissful, we are seriously committed to each other and to our life together.

Her boyfriend was at that very moment flying in from out of town to spend his one free day with her.

As his plane landed, her heart began to flutter. Eager anticipation showed all over her face as her cheeks grew pink and her eyes shone. An elderly couple poked each other as the wife whispered, "Young love. It's so splendid!"

The old man hugged his wife and whispered, "So is old love, honey. I still love you."

Her wrinkled cheeks grew pink and her elderly eyes shone. Just then the young woman's boyfriend rushed out, yelled out her name and swooped her up with joy. Everyone around smiled at the two sets of lovers — so different, so alike.

• • • • • • • •

My greatest joy would be to stay in love
over the years, through all the trials,
tribulations and laughter, and still
adore each other decades later.

Loving another person can be wonderful. In fact, it is often one of life's greatest pleasures. Yet many times we fail at love over and over again, and we don't have a clue why.

In truth, the most important love is self-love, the ability to respect our needs, goals and desires and to take care of ourselves. Without self-love, a person cannot be emotionally ready to love another person.

We can love ourselves without being egocentric or selfish. In fact, self-love demonstrates respect for who we are and what we need in life.

· · · · · · · ·

Damaged in childhood, it has been hard for me to learn to trust and love myself. I am now ready to begin an unselfish adult relationship for the first time in my life.

So many of us have heard these famous words. The phrase, "Trust me, I know what is good for you," has caught more than one of us in a relationship we wish we'd never started.

It's relatively easy to be thrown off guard by someone who is really handsome or beautiful, by a person who seems smarter or more educated, or by one who seems more worldly than we are.

In fact, we are the only person who really knows what is good for us. But sometimes we are so overwhelmed by our need to be in love, to be attached to another person, to get out of the singles scene — especially with a person who is good-looking and intelligent — that we forget our own needs.

· · · · · · · ·

When someone says, "Trust me,"
I've learned through hard experience I
had better not. I will trust myself
and my intuition instead.

If we married very young, it's likely that we hadn't yet reached full emotional maturity. Many marital unions fall apart, not because the two people are no longer in love, but because one grows and the other does not. Marriages that happen among the very young are not usually made in heaven.

In order to preserve love and commitment, each person must be willing to grow and mature and not stay "frozen" at the same stage of maturity where they were at the time of their wedding.

Keeping current with world affairs, attending college to get a degree, taking community education classes for personal enrichment or getting promoted to a position of more responsibility — not to speak of parenting children — all will enhance maturity and let both people grow at their own rate.

· · · · · · · ·

We both continue to grow, not necessarily
in the same way, and as we do, our love
continues to grow as well.

It happens to every one of us at some time or another. We get frightened. Perhaps it is a new job, or moving to a new city, or maybe we have been involved with someone for years and it's suddenly over.

Not surprisingly, even when the adult in us looks competent and self-assured, our Inner Child can still get frightened. We each carry that small child in us, the one who is afraid to tackle something new lest we do it wrong.

Dating may well provoke the old fears and bring forth our insecure Inner Child. Acting "as if" we feel comfortable will help us learn to actually feel comfortable. Then our Inner Child will settle down and maybe even give us a hand.

. . . .

I need to introduce my adult self to my
Inner Child and hope that they
will get along with each other.

From bi-coastal marriages to professions that require selling on the road, being apart when you are in love can be really hard. Even though this lifestyle might not be one we would have chosen, true love should be strong enough to survive the separations.

Letting the one we love do his or her job without anger or hurt on our part is an important gift we can each give to the other. Hearing, "I'll be waiting for you, and remember I love you," can be the ember that keeps our heart warm during those long periods when the one we share our life and love with is gone.

· · · · · · · ·

While I am lonely without my loved one,
I am strong enough to handle
my loneliness.

Being single again is a double-edged sword. On the one hand, we are free to pursue a new social life if we wish. On the other hand, we are not exactly certain how to proceed. For those of us who have been attached to the same person for more than ten years, dating is but a distant memory.

If we do want to move on, to get back into the social scene, then it may help if we ask friends or colleagues who have already gone through the experience. We'll be pleased and surprised that most people are willing to share some helpful hints about dating again.

It takes a truly courageous person to admit they need help and that they have no idea how or where to begin. Asking for help is not a sign of personal weakness, but instead of great strength.

• • • • • • • •

My hidden strengths are surfacing with great frequency now that I am alone. I am so proud of myself.

April 17	*Successful Change*

It is hard to accept change. We sometimes cling to old habits just because we are uncertain what our life would be like if we were to change. Beginning anew as a single person can be a frightening and uncertain time of life.

People who make it through the changes which do occur in their lives when the one they used to love is not living with them any longer — when the love has ended for whatever reason — are the ones who have been able to accept changes in life as they have grown up and moved along with living.

Those who can move on, who want to move on, are likely to be the most successful ones at any type of life transition. Beginning new relationships offers wonderful new opportunities.

• • • • • • • •

*Accepting change is not easy for me, but once
I tried I was pleased to find I can
handle changes in my life.*

Somehow John, with his cockeyed sense of humor, his slightly rotund body and his unmanageable cowlick, crept up on Julie. When she wasn't even trying to become involved again, she found herself very much in love with the most unlikely match to her businesslike, no-nonsense personality.

Actually, the person we marry should really be our best friend. The one who loves us and we love back should be the one who sticks with us through thick and thin, who laughs at our jokes when they have been heard 20 times before and whose face still lights up when we enter a room.

Best friends forever. Best friends to share all of our adult lives. What a nice thought.

• • • • • • • •

For my second time around
I have been careful to choose a person
not for what they do, but
for who they are.

Some of us don't like ourselves very much. In fact, we like and respect ourselves so little that we think, "It's no wonder no one loves me. There's isn't much to love." This self-defeating attitude indicates very low self-esteem and can only serve to perpetuate itself unless the cycle is finally broken.

Before we rush out to meet new "possibles" — men or women in similar situations looking to date and maybe even to become serious — perhaps we need to learn to enjoy our own company and to spend time alone without criticizing our actions.

This is no easy task. But until we succeed in being totally comfortable with ourselves, until we no longer make excuses for how we look and why we act the way we do, we are likely to have yet another unsatisfactory love.

• • • • • • • •

I will not be hurt again. Before I begin to date, I will work on learning to be comfortable with myself.

Life, they say, is what happens while we are waiting for something else. For some reason, even if we are not in a romantic attachment, some of us wait for our Prince or Princess Charming to sweep us off our feet. We may wait all our lives and not find anyone to love.

But we can move on, get going and figure out what went wrong last time so we can make it better the next time around. Then we can get to work on our problems so we won't be just waiting. Instead we'll be doing, fixing, learning and beginning anew.

By not waiting for the special person to appear on our doorstep, by not waiting for magic, we can learn about ourselves and go out with a light heart to meet new friends.

• • • • • • • •

The child in me still believes in magic.
My adult side knows there can be magic sometimes,
but I need to create my own.

Most of us know that queasy feeling of anxiety. Our stomachs churn, we may get a headache, or palms get sweaty and we might even feel light-headed. Having been involved with one person for a long while, we may well feel anxious when faced with the prospect of dating again. It helps to analyze why we feel the way we do.

In fact, it could be that we are not comfortable with who we are or with how we represent ourselves. Are we happy? Are we content with ourselves? If not, it is time to do some self-work.

It is only through making peace with ourselves — by feeling totally comfortable — that we can step out to greet the world on our terms.

• • • • • • • •

Getting ready to date again presents a marvelous
opportunity for me to grow. I know
the time is right for me.

It really can be a wonderful time of life. Children finally grown and moved out. The problem is that some of us aren't sure how to treat our adult children once they are gone. We were used to having teenagers in the house, complete with clutter and mess.

If we had a special man or woman in our lives, we even got used to being cautious around the kids. As they grew older, we had to learn to respect each other's privacy.

Now we have to formulate a new set of rules — how to act around our adult children. Most of us welcome the end of parenting and relish the beginning of adult relationships with our own children. For a while it may feel uncomfortable, but soon we will fall into the pattern of treating our children as adults.

• • • • • • • •

Looking at my children through different eyes,
I see young adults who are trying hard to build their
own lives. I will take my cue from them
and begin to rebuild mine as well.

A popular song tells of a person who is ". . . looking for love in all the wrong places." Unfortunately, we may be doing the very same thing without even realizing it. After all, we are ready to date again, right?

As youths we met people to date at parties, perhaps at singles bars or maybe at school. It wouldn't be appropriate now to go to the same places we did many years ago. Instead, we rely on friends to fix us up, join groups where singles might attend and develop new interests where we might meet some new friends.

Rather than looking for love, we understand that what we are looking for first is friendship. If love happens after a while, then we have received a wonderful bonus.

• • • • • • • •

I am not looking for a lover,
but instead for a person who will be my friend,
whom I can eventually fall in love with
and who will share my love.

In our dreams we were always handsome or beautiful, youthful, happy and full of vigor. Such is the idealism of youth.

Sometimes things happen in life we never could have imagined in our wildest dreams. Our lifestyle can totally change due to altered health. We've depended on being well for so long that making the adjustment — and subsequently working to stay in love with the same person — seems nearly impossible at first. Illness does happen, but it's not anything we bargained for.

After careful consideration some people choose to stay in the relationship or marriage. Others leave. There is no way to call the shots ahead of time. Sometimes ill health is more than we can bear.

· · · · · · · · ·

I know things can't be the same between us,
but that doesn't mean we can't find a compromise.
We can decide what is best for our relationship
and act on those thoughts.

Ultimately many of us wind up alone. Alone because the one we loved has passed on. Alone because we choose to be. Alone because our marriage has ended. Alone because all the children have gone. That's not a situation many of us would have wished for.

But until we learn to enjoy our own company, until we find it comfortable to be just with ourselves, we will not be emotionally ready to fall in love again. Feeling completely comfortable alone takes the urgency out of finding another person to love.

In the end we rely on ourselves for emotional strength and fortitude, and hopefully we are able to love ourselves.

• • • • • • • •

I am happy with myself and
feel comfortable that I am ready to share
my joy with someone else.

Some people have problems during childhood and young adulthood with disruptive attention-getting behavior, with drinking or with the use of drugs. Luckily they straighten out and become stable and responsible adults.

Occasionally these people revert back to old negative behaviors. Why does this happen after years of being good husbands or wives and responsible community members?

Sometimes people in adulthood become frightened by how much they have become responsible for. Their job. Their spouse. Their children. Yet it's always such a surprise when they do well for years and then have trouble again. As small children would, they use their negative behaviors as a way to hide in their own emotional closet.

· · · · · · · ·

I understand that my loved one may need professional help, and I will work hard to cooperate and offer support at this difficult time in our lives.

There are so many ways for one person to love another. From parental love to brotherly love, from impassioned love to spiritual love, we offer our undevoted love to one another.

Sometimes love is equal and healthy. But sometimes love is unhealthy. In co-dependent love we encourage and enable behaviors such as drinking, use of drugs and physical or emotional abuse, very likely without recognizing we are encouraging this behavior.

Until we recognize that our behavior is adding directly to and even helping to cause our loved one's problems, we won't do anything about it. Once we do, there are any number of groups and books available to offer us help. We are not responsible for anyone's behavior but our own.

· · · · · · · ·

Now that I have found some help, I recognize that the way I gave love was harmful. I am working to change my own behavior.

118

Of course how we re-enter the dating world matters a great deal to us. But what matters even more is whether we make ourselves stay in the dating game even if it appears we are not winning.

Not having dated for a good many years, many of us start timidly, as if putting one toe into the ocean to test the water's temperature.

Beginning matters a great deal, especially to those of us who are nervous about trying again. But staying with it, persisting until we do begin to make some new friends and renew old ones, until we do start dating again, will help us feel good about ourselves, about how desirable we are and about our own sense of self-worth.

· · · · · · · ·

While I am all right alone, I do not
want aloneness to become a permanent state
of affairs in my life. I want to
be in love again.

"She's a fake," Betty whispered to Paul. "She acts like she thinks she is terrific."

"Personally," he answered, "I don't think anything is wrong with acting that way. She's not hurting anyone. And if a person acts the way they would really like everyone to see them, it may soon become truth."

The next time Betty went to a party, she decided to try his theory for herself. She felt very nervous, but she acted self-assured.

To Betty's surprise, his system worked. Different people she knew came over to her during the course of the evening and asked questions like, "Did you get your hair cut?" and "Are you wearing a new dress?" No one could figure out what had happened to Betty. But she and her husband knew and they were happy the idea had worked.

• • • • • • • •

If I act self-assured, people will think
I really am. The more assured
they think I am, the more assured I feel.

"I must be a bad person. Neither of my marriages worked," lamented Dorothy to her friend Emily. "I don't know what's wrong with me."

Emily smiled and said, "Why don't you try turning around what you just said? Reframe it in different words. For example, why not say 'He was not a good person. He had many problems.' Or even better try, 'I am a good person. There is nothing wrong with me. I just happened to have been involved in two unhappy marriages.' "

Dorothy slowly began to smile. "Thank you, Emily. What you just shared with me casts a whole new light on things."

. . . .

I do not need to accept
all the blame for a failed relationship.
I am a good person.

It's a sad story but one often told. A man or a woman has come through an unhappy marriage. Unhappy because their personalities just didn't meld. Unhappy because of verbal or physical abuse. Unhappy because of vast and irreconcilable differences in their family's social status and background.

So the marriage splits up. Not usually because it was abominable, but more often because it never grew comfortable the way an old shoe becomes comfortable.

When the time comes and the newly single person feels ready to date again, he or she needs to do some thinking. What is good for me? What do I need and want in a relationship?

. . . .

*I respect myself and value
my personal needs.*

It feels exciting and perhaps a bit frightening to re-enter the world of dating. Single again, we really don't feel quite ready to conquer the world. As we begin to date, we feel we are ready to become involved again — ready to fall in love.

If we enter the dating world with the attitude of "finding" the right person, we may be doomed to failure from the start. Some available single people are scared away when they realize that one's intention is marriage.

Talking about commitment and marriage on the first date can be frightening. Instead, the goal should be to have fun, to enjoy the one we are dating.

. . . .

Even though I want to get married again,
I realize for my own sake that I need
to be cautious and move slowly.

"Now, don't forget, Corey," his father warned, "you married badly last time. Try not to repeat your mistake, son." Corey was annoyed by his father's advice.

"Dad, there was no way I could know it wouldn't work when we got married. You're not being fair. How would I have known?"

Corey's father then went on to explain that it was evident to everyone but his son that they were mismatched. He was so stricken with his ex-wife's beauty and her dependence upon him that he couldn't understand how hard marriage would be with a completely dependent person.

• • • • • • • •

I will not settle for less or compromise my own needs; I will enter a relationship with my eyes fully open.

Being in love is one of the most joyful experiences of life. Falling out of love is often one of the saddest. We have a hard time realizing that our relationship is no more. We still expect the person we used to love to come around the corner any moment.

Now we have a second chance. We begin to realize there are other people with whom we might also be happy. We begin to date, perhaps just a bit at first. Then, if it is what we want, we start to date seriously, to look in earnest for the right person whom we will love and who will love us back.

Being in love again is one of the most joyful experiences in life. Realizing that we love a person who loves us back, who is kind and warm and believes in equality in marriage, is one of the most joyful moments life has to offer.

· · · · · · · · ·

Joy fills my life and lifts my spirits.
I am loved and I am lovable.

Practically the moment after the divorce papers were finalized, Herb raced out to the telephone to call Cindy, a flight attendant he had met on his flight back from Hawaii. She was quite pretty and very friendly, and she had willingly given Herb her home phone number.

Cindy agreed to meet him for dinner at a nearby steak house. They ordered and began to talk. Or at least Herb began to talk. Cindy listened. And listened. And listened. "Herb," she said finally "do you know that all you have talked about is your ex-wife?

"I suggest you wait a few weeks before you date again. It's no fun to go out with a person who talks about someone else all evening. You need to get over the loss from your divorce before you date again."

. . . .

Wanting too much too soon helped me
pause and reflect on my life, which then helped
me decide which direction I want to go.

A warning flag should automatically rise when you are asked out by a person over 40 or so, male or female, who has never been married. This is not to say anything is wrong, but it might be.

When dating a never-married person, it is wise to progress slowly. Before too long you will find out why they have not yet been married. The reasons could vary from having lost a loved one in an accident or to illness, to still living with a parent, to not ever having found the "right" person to marry.

The problem often is that no person has been "right" enough, that no one has been "good enough" to meet this person's standards, or perhaps the standards of their parents.

. . . .

I need to look out for my own needs when I date a "never married" person. If no one has ever been good enough for them, I can choose not to join the competition.

It used to happen more often with men than with women. These days it seems to be equal. We have all met them. The "Great Pretenders," people who claim to be what they are not.

Some try to look classy and act wealthy; others may feign a college degree or job. Sometimes the pretense is blatant and anyone can tell. At other times it is so finely tuned, the pretender turns out to be a con artist.

A relationship should always be based on complete and total honesty. If it starts with one person pretending to be something they are not, true love is unlikely to develop.

· · · · · · · ·

I am who I am and proud of it.
I need no pretense to feel
good about myself.

All of the people we date have their own personality quirks and have developed their own individual ways of coping with the issues surrounding being single. Their coping mechanisms range from being slightly beyond normal to outright bizarre.

In fact, we all have developed coping skills for being single — whether we are newly single or permanently single. What matters is whether our quirks impose themselves on our interactions with other people in such a way that it puts them off.

It's not a bad idea to examine how "quirky" our personalities are if we find ourselves rarely being asked out for a second or third time. If we are uncomfortable with our self-discovery, it may be time for some personal change.

· · · · · · · ·

I now understand that it is not always
the other person who is different. It is time for
me to take a serious personality inventory
and act upon my shortcomings.

When you are dating someone who seems really important to you — someone with whom you may be considering sharing your life — there is an almost foolproof way to check on how that person is viewed by others who don't know him or her very well.

Take the person you are dating home to a big family dinner or to dinner with a group of old friends. The one you think you love may absolutely shine — using polite manners, treating you nicely, even telling a few tasteful jokes.

On the other hand, that same person may make such a fool out of themselves that you would like to creep away forever. Being with friends and family when the person's guard is really down will help you find the "real" person.

• • • • • • • •

It has been said, "The true test
of love is how you are treated in front of family.
However you are treated then is a good indicator
of how you will be treated in the future."

Occasionally, as we dine with friends in a restaurant, we notice people who are eating alone. Noticing no wedding ring, we may start to speculate. One might say, "Maybe he is out of town on business."

Another speculates, "Maybe the poor person just wants to be alone."

In fact, some people have chosen a life of solitude, but there is often a good reason for their choice. Perhaps they have been hurt physically or emotionally by someone they used to love. Maybe they just prefer being alone. The reasons are many and varied.

The key is to always respect a person's need to be alone — in fact, to even really be a loner. While being alone happens to some by default, others may choose it as their permanent lifestyle.

· · · · · · · ·

There is no need for me to try to "fix" a person's
aloneness. I respect each person's right to
choose their own lifestyle.

Years ago there was a glut of media information cautioning us not to invade another's personal space. Most of us learned our lesson well, recognizing that to stand too close while talking to another feels uncomfortable and intrusive.

Needless to say, there are times when the "rules" should be broken, such as when lovers are being sexually intimate. Otherwise we shouldn't forget that the personal space boundaries come right back into play after the moments of intimacy are over.

No one wants to share their every thought and action with another person, even if they are deeply in love. We all deserve the right to be private, even to be a bit secretive about our own thoughts and feelings.

· · · · · · · ·

One important ingredient that makes our love work is that we both deeply respect each other's right to privacy.

How we feel when we break up with a person we loved deeply is hard to describe. Hurt. Upset. Angry. Betrayed. Maybe even relieved. Emotions can run rampant during this emotionally precarious time of life.

Eventually we gain our sense of perspective. We begin to really remember why it ended and recognize that it was only partly our fault, if at all. It takes a long while to face the truth and to be ready to move on in life.

When the time comes that we do enter into the social mainstream again, it will be easier if we try to "put away" our old baggage — to store it in our memory bank to be opened later if we need it. If we can begin dating again with an open mind, a clear head and a good feeling about ourselves, we stand a much better chance to enjoy this wonderful new phase of our life.

• • • • • • • •

Finally I am looking forward to dating again.
My past failure will not overshadow my enjoyment.
I am okay now, and I am ready.

When we have been hurt, when our life has been turned topsy-turvy by ending a marriage or love affair, looking into our future seems an impossible task. No one wants to imagine themselves alone 20 years from now.

With that thought in mind, too many are frantic to begin dating again with the ultimate goal being marriage. This attitude tends to scare prospective dates away. Looking only toward the end goal — not being alone — just doesn't work when we begin to date again.

Instead, it is gentler and easier if at first we take one day at a time. Set goals for just one day. Perhaps one goal might be to become involved in a neighborhood class to meet new friends, both male and female. Signing up for the class is the first step. Plan just one day at a time. Life will start to feel manageable once again.

· · · · · · · ·

Easy does it. I will be fine if I don't try to project my life 20 years from now.

Children from unhappy homes, especially where there was drinking, drug use, verbal abuse or physical abuse, developed their personality patterns at home. If those same children had been raised in strong and stable homes, they would have developed completely different.

As we enter new relationships, we bring along our old behaviors. In fact, we may unconsciously choose people to date because they feel familiar to us. If they feel comfortable because they act like one of our parents did and we fall back into negative childhood roles, we'd better look at why.

If, however, we feel comfortable because we are treated with respect, because we are treated warmly yet not violated personally, then we are indeed lucky.

· · · · · · · ·

I don't have to date anyone who makes me feel uncomfortable. I have changed, and I am emotionally strong now.

Just one extra small piece of candy. It really won't matter in the overall scheme of things, we reason to ourselves. Yet in truth it does. If weight is a personal issue, each small piece of candy eaten entices us to deceive ourselves a bit more.

Most of us deceive ourselves at some time or another in life. More than one of us has said, "I wouldn't act the way I do if my father had cared about me," or "It's my husband's fault. I wouldn't have been shoplifting if he'd told me he loved me more often."

It isn't that we set out intending to deceive ourselves, but sometimes the truth hurts so much we avoid acknowledging that we have caused many of our own problems. Until we recognize that fact and either own up to our behavior or get some professional help, we will continue to be self-deceptive.

· · · · · · · ·

My behavior is my own. I will not blame anyone for the way I choose to act.

No one wants to be beholden to another person — financially, emotionally or physically. Yet too often we find ourselves in a situation where we are dependent upon another person for our well-being.

In every long-term relationship there is occasionally some dependency — but not co-dependency — which occurs. One person may be ill and need help for a while from the other. One may lose a job and not be able to contribute to family finances for a time. But it all should equal out in the end.

For example, when one partner gets all of their gratification socially from the other, then something is wrong in their relationship. Each of us should be autonomous, able to function in life without the "crutch" of a loved one at our side. If we can't, then we need to take a long, hard look at our life and our lifestyle.

• • • • • • • •

My need to lean on another person has diminished as I have grown strong within myself.

When two people love each other and
have a committed relationship, the act of
lovemaking is a natural outpouring of their
mutual feelings. But for some of us the very
thought of talking with our partner about
the act of sex gives us the chills.

Unless we openly communicate with our
lover, we will not get what we want sexually.
Some people want more, others less. Some
liked to be touched in one place but not in
another.

Learning to talk openly about sex will
help. Say, "I like it when . . . ," or "it makes
me uncomfortable when you . . ." Try, "Let's
spend more time on foreplay," or "I like to be
held after we make love." It isn't that the one
we love is insensitive to our needs. But if we
don't talk about what we need, the other will
assume everything is fine the way it is.

. . . .

Assumptions are not fair to either one of us.
We both can talk openly about what we
would like during the act of love.

138

Small issues become larger issues if we don't talk about them. We fight sometimes about the strangest things. "I can't stand it when you leave the toilet seat up, and why don't you ever wash your hair off the soap?"

"Well, you never squeeze the toothpaste tube right or put away your dirty underwear!" These seem trivial reasons to fight, yet they often escalate into full-blown arguments.

There are solutions to these squabbles. Perhaps buying two tubes of toothpaste would help, or picking up your loved one's underwear if he or she does one extra load of laundry each week. By looking for the humor in our daily struggles as a couple and finding solutions by compromise, it is likely the reasons we fought at all will suddenly disappear.

• • • • • • • •

By learning to step back from the argument and look for the solutions first, I can avert many bitter words in our relationship.

To many the term "conference" sounds threatening, something one might be called to the boss's office for. To others, the words conference conjures up memories of being chastised by their parents when they were young.

There is yet another way to look at the term conference. Two people who love each other, married or not, can ask to set aside a specific time during the next few days when they can talk. This is done without anger and should not be threatening in any way.

From talking about their relationship to their financial situation to helping another family member or friend in need, conferencing is an ideal non-threatening way to discuss something of major importance.

• • • • • • • •

I do not ask for a conference in a fit of anger, but instead ask as a realistic and mature way to deal with problems.

Remember the old saying, "Too many cooks in the kitchen spoil the broth?" Some people believe this is true. It can be, but only if the person who is doing the cooking — or the work in the garage or the painting — doesn't want the other person to be there.

Realistically, there can be real joy and gratification in sharing a job with a person we love. Granted, too much togetherness is not good if one person is always correcting or goading the other.

However, if the two people can work together, side by side — as all relationships should ideally be — then the presence of one can enhance the enjoyment and behavior of the other.

· · · · · · · ·

Having a person who wants to share my life,
my kitchen and my work makes
me the lucky one.

While we may not realize it, one of the most important facets of any relationship, whether with a boss, a dear friend, a family member or a person whom we love deeply, is to feel validated.

Simple words of praise or understanding such as, "That was a really good idea," or "I can understand your viewpoint better now," make us feel important and valuable. The opposite approach can make us feel small, childlike and unimportant.

Being validated by what we do, by how others perceive us and even how we look to the world in general can only serve to enhance our maturity and self-respect.

• • • • • • • •

Being validated or validating another person
is one case for the celebration of life.

No one is perfect. No one person is always right. We each carry our entire life's background and all our past understanding to every situation.

When we think we know it all, that no one is better than we are, that no one can do anything as well as we can, we are missing an essential quality of life — humility. Humility is not an easily-learned lesson if it is not taught to us in childhood.

The person who is humble accepts the will of a Higher Power and understands that expressing humility is a sign of deep internal strength, not at all a sign of external weakness.

· · · · · · · ·

*Being humble is being willing to show
that humility is the hallmark of
a wise and mature person.*

My, how fast we work and live these days! Hurry, hurry, everywhere we go. Hurry to work, to pick up the children, to rush to the store or to get in the right amount of daily exercise. There are never enough minutes in our day.

So much work leaves too little time to play. When we forget to play, life ceases to be fun. Play should not end when we become old enough to go to work. Yet far too many use the precious weekend time to clean house, run to the bank and dry cleaners and do yard work.

Life needs to be regrouped so there is a small amount of time each day and even more on the weekend to play. To sit and talk. To go for a walk or to the zoo. To see a movie or a play or have a picnic. Half play and half work make a balanced life.

· · · · · · · ·

*For a while I forgot to play and
my life became unbalanced. Now I remember the
purity of time spent just playing.*

People sometimes get confused about what balance of power really means. Balance of power is quite different from empowerment, yet both must be present in order to keep growing in a relationship.

Balance of power means that in a marriage or in a long-term love sometimes one person will be stronger in one specific area while the other might have completely different strengths. In the long haul, however, they are approximately equal and their strengths and weak points balance out.

Empowerment is the sense of personal strength that does not depend upon anyone else. A person who is empowered is not particulary strong physically, but very strong emotionally.

· · · · · · · ·

*After my love ended, I felt deflated and a bit
worthless. As time passed, I recognized
that I am the same strong person
I always was, and I will be fine.*

Conflict. What a harsh word that can be. We imagine ourselves in conflict with another person — an immovable force perhaps. But this is not always true. Conflict can often be resolved with compromise — by talking together to create a whole new level of understanding.

Being in conflict can be personal, as we can sometimes be in conflict with ourselves. Conflict often occurs before a fight and can be a couple's early warning signal for trouble on their horizon.

Conflict can be a call to arms for a knock-down, drag-out fight or a stepping stone to cross to a deeper level of understanding each other.

· · · · · · · ·

I choose to use conflict as a stepping stone
to greater awareness of my needs
and the needs of others.

If you were to ask 100 people to define intimacy, most of them would use the word sex in their definition. Yet this is not the whole truth. Certainly sex does play a role in intimacy — but just one role.

A couple who are really close are intimate on many levels. They share spiritual intimacy when they both worship their God. They may share the intimacy, which seems to happen automatically when one has children.

They share their days and their nights and they talk about their life together. Not fight. Intimate, warm and caring talk. Intimacy, of course, occurs during sex as well, but many people report that they feel closer to their loved one when they are talking face to face than when they are making love.

• • • • • • • •

With mutual respect and caring and a great deal of conversation our intimate moments will occur more and more often.

Wow, it sure can be hard to be in love. So much happens that seems destined to keep us from finding the right person and dating long enough to really get close and to finally fall in love.

During every love, each one of us hits huge potholes in the road of life or finds molehills too high to jump over. We have two choices. If we can't stand the heat, we'll just put out the fire. And so the love simmers down, burns out and then ends.

But there are other options. We can deal with our problems. We can wait them out, talk them over or get professional help. Many marriages that end in divorce could have made it if there had been help. Breaking up is not the only solution. Many people break up in haste and are sorry later.

• • • • • • • •

Time and talking, along with hugging and caring, often can heal even the deepest wounds.

Love can be so wonderful and so glorious that we sometimes lose sight of the fact that we are more in love with the idea of being in love than with the person we are actually dating. We start to find fault and pick the other person apart in our mind.

In order for the relationship to move forward, we need to look at all our options. Do we love this person? Is this someone we would like to spend our lifetime with? Do we respect this person? If the answers are mostly yes, then we need to take the time to reframe the relationship on new terms so both people will feel happy and satisfied.

If not, it may be time to make the break and move forward. This is a giant step to take, and when we do, we will leave our love behind. If we are ready to move on, then that person was not right for us in the first place.

• • • • • • • •

I want to be in love, to be part of a couple again, but it must be with a person who is right for me.

Remember junior high school? Remember when someone started a nasty rumor that followed a poor innocent person around the whole year? We were capable of doing such cruel and insensitive things to other kids when we were young.

Now that we are older, some of us still do something almost as hurtful. We gossip about other people. Without even taking the time to verify the information, we pass on the story we have just heard, perhaps even taking time to embellish it just a bit. Gossip is just a rumor dressed in an adult's clothing.

Gossiping about another person just isn't fair. If the person is really a close friend, most of us wouldn't consider breaking our promise of confidence. And if they are not, perhaps we would serve them better not to pass on stories we can't verify.

· · · · · · · ·

*I respect my friendships too much
to jeopardize them with
vicious gossip.*

Breaking up or getting divorced is cause for celebration for some people, but for others it is the beginning of a long period of sadness. Self-worth plunges to an all-time low, and we may even sink into a blue funk.

Feeling sad for a period of time is normal. Sometimes we need to wallow in our own self-pity. Maybe for a whole weekend we stay in bed, watch TV, never shower and only eat food that is not good for us.

But if we can't shake our sadness, then depression may be the culprit. People often need help working through depression. Unlike sadness, depression can't just be shaken off with one weekend of self-pity. Professional help will be invaluable. Soon we will be able to face the world with a genuine smile.

. . . .

*While I may not want to date again
for a long while, I can function once
again quite normally.*

Sitting right near the telephone, we remind anyone who wants to use it that we are expecting a very special person to call. Every time the phone rings our heart gives a little lurch. Finally, the call comes, and we smile from ear to ear.

The anticipation from such a phone call has been experienced by nearly all of us at one time or another. It is the wonderful and unique feeling of being in love — or at least the feeling of being in very strong "like."

Eventually, as the relationship progresses, we do settle down. It's a good thing, too, since none of our bodies would be able to handle the adrenaline rush every time the telephone rings. Once the high of new love dissipates, we need to decide whether this person has enough in common with us to stay for a lifetime.

· · · · · · · ·

New love and true love are both parts of
the whole process. I want to move past new love in
order to develop true and lasting love.

Recovery. We are used to hearing the word bandied about these days. Recovery from alcohol abuse. Recovery from overeating. Recovery from drug addiction. Recovery talk is a new part of nearly everyone's vocabulary these days.

But we also need to remember that the word recovery has other meanings as well. It takes time to recover from a broken love affair or marriage. Giving ourselves the time we need is invaluable — a type of self-gift. We can't be rushed to heal when we feel broken.

Recovery can be slow, since parting from a loved one often leaves us bruised and battered. However, the journey can also be one of growth and excitement as we discover our new strengths and eventually develop a new zest for living.

• • • • • • • •

The gift of time is one I can well afford.
I must heal before I can try again.

Being alone is often expressed as one of the greatest fears a person has after their love or marriage has broken up. In fact, some people continue to call their ex-boyfriends or ex-wives just to hear that once-so-familiar voice.

Recognizing, finally, that it is really and truly over, we stop calling, stop the imaginary calls and stop writing letters we never mail. We start depending on our own strengths a little more. This is hard work. The thought of living our life without sharing it with someone we love is downright terrifying to most of us.

Instead of worrying about the long haul, set short goals at first. Worry about the coming weekend instead of the one three years from now. Make plans with friends or investigate places in your city where you have not gone before.

. . . .

A person is alone only if they don't reach out for others. I need not be alone.

It can feel as though someone we loved dearly has died. In fact, those very words, "It is over. This is just not going to work," can stab our heart emotionally with the same great sense of loss.

We talk about the demise of a person in death, yet we rarely talk about the demise of a person in life. Demise. What a strange word. The demise of our love. The word suddenly feels correct.

Demise. Such a dramatic word to discuss the end of love. Demise. The end of something we thought would last forever. It takes a long time to accept the demise of our love.

• • • • • • • •

When I am finally ready to step out,
to try again, I know I have
successfully put the demise of my
relationship behind me.

Often when a certain age in life comes and goes — usually betwen 25 and 35 — people become frightened that they may never find the right mate. Everywhere they turn it seems there is another friend who has just become engaged.

We begin to wonder if we are destined to spend our lives alone, with no one to love, with no children and no extended family. If we let ourselves get caught up in fear, we may have a tendency to compromise our ideals and date or marry someone who is less than the type of person we envision. Of course, it's also entirely possible that we have designed a person so perfect in our mind that this person can never exist in reality.

We can look actively for a mate, through dating services, by taking classes, through work and by asking friends to fix us up.

. . . .

True love will not come knocking at my door.
Sometimes I have to meet it halfway.

We smiled our way through childhood, even when we felt so unhappy we would have liked to curl up under our covers and stay there forever. We hid our anger often in order to maintain our sometimes precarious family position.

That anger often stayed buried and never did find a way to get expressed. And further, if we didn't learn how to be angry as children, we may be quite frightened of showing anger as an adult. If a person we love yells at us, we recoil or even cry, certain our love is over and that we have done something wrong.

It seems strange that we must learn we have the right to be mad and to say so, just as long as we don't abuse another person. Being angry on occasion is a healthy way to vent our emotions.

• • • • • • • •

Anger is a healthy emotion.
It helps keep my life in balance.

Sometimes we want more than anything else in the world to look, be and act like the people who surround us. Yet no matter how hard we try, we just can't seem to make the grade.

From childhood on, being accepted is one of our major goals. Yet it seems we were the last person chosen in gym to be on the team, the last one to start dating and even the last one to fall in love.

This negative outlook on life can be changed though we act as though we have the right to be like everyone else — that in fact, we are like everyone else. If we were to look around, we would be surprised to find far more similarities than differences.

· · · · · · · ·

My body language can be positive and happy,
even if I don't feel that way at first. Soon it
will become habit and I will begin to
think better of myself.

Teenagers worry about it all the time. "I'm a geek! There is nothing about me that is normal. I have huge pimples. My hair looks funny. I'm too short!" Both girls and boys lament their shortcomings, without enough maturity to recognize that they will grow and their pimples will disappear.

Now we are alone — single again, and our old teenage fears creep in once more. "No one likes me. Who would ever want to go out with me? I'm no prize to look at."

We can either laugh at ourselves for falling into our old behavior or move on, understanding fully that other newly single people suffer exactly the way we are suffering.

· · · · · · · ·

Stopping negative self-talk and reminding myself I am worthy, I am fun and I can make new friends will help me move on with my life.

Sometimes the very thought of starting to date and perhaps becoming serious is enough to cause a feeling of excitement.

We need to take time to consider that our need to be with someone — anyone — can cloud our good judgment. Our lifelong goals need to be weighed at this time. Would the person we are dating possibly fit into our future plans and goals? Could we fit into theirs? Is he or she gentle and warm, intelligent and motivated?

These questions and more need to be mulled over before we let the feelings of our heart overtake the realities we recognize in our mind. If it seems wrong, don't do it. A person who seems too good to be true just might be. Wait a while. Give your new relationship some time to grow.

• • • • • • • •

While I eagerly anticipate being committed once again to a person I love, I care enough about myself to take my time and make sure it's right.

Even if we have worked out our personal problems through therapy or group work, we may inadvertently find ourselves attracted to a person who does not have a good history of staying with the person they love.

Unfortunately, it has long been known that a person's past performance is a strong predictor of their future performance. Unless something has happened — such as personal growth — they will repeat old mistakes over and over.

The problem is that these are basically nice people who can usually sweet-talk the husk off a cob of corn. We want to be liked, we need to be loved and we want to believe they are telling the truth. If you are dating a person who has already had several relationship failures in the past, run — don't walk — to the nearest exit.

. . . .

I don't want to become the latest in a long series of conflicts and affairs. I will leave this harmful relationship before it really begins.

Dating a person who really seems to care about us answers one of our most basic human needs — our need to feel secure. We all like to feel secure about our lives, about having our needs met and about being in love.

The sense of security we get from a good strong relationship is a wonderful feeling. It's like finding a pair of shoes that fit perfectly and need no breaking in. We feel comfortable. We feel at home. And most importantly, we feel at ease both with ourselves and with our love.

Security is an important and basic need. Knowing that the one we adore loves us right back can only serve to enhance the sense of security we feel when we have fallen in love with the right person.

· · · · · · · ·

Our love felt good at the beginning.
Our love feels even more secure months later.
I love being in love.

In every relationship there are boundaries. As children we knew just how far we could push our parents and when to zip out of the room before we caused real trouble. We knew how to act in synagogue or church and how to act in school.

The same is true when two people are in love. Each one of us establishes our own personal boundaries. For example, one person might need a brief time to be alone after work just to unwind. Another might ask that no one touch the pile of mail until it has been sorted and read by them only.

Boundaries. Some are reasonable and some are not. If they don't work for us, we need to sit down and find a good compromise or at least understand why our loved one has set them.

. . . .

We each need private space and private time. I respect each person's boundaries and hope they will respect mine as well.

Strange as it seems, there are different levels of equality. What is equal for one may not necessarily feel equal for another. Some families may work out their equality in a somewhat sexist way while others share equally, choosing to work side by side.

Many people enter a relationship with an unrealistic idea of what marriage is like. They choose their partner on the basis of their own personal needs. Some women choose men they can mother or men similar to their fathers so they can get more fathering. Men may choose to be mothered.

Whatever the reason, too many people unconsciously choose people to parent or who will parent them, rather than choosing to share life equally.

· · · · · · · ·

Aware that so many marriages fail,
my eyes are fully open to the potential
problem of inequality.

Many people moved from their parent's home to college and right into marriage. They never had the experience of living on their own or making their own decisions. They never learned that cooking, budgeting and running a household are not easy chores.

If you were to enter a marriage or a live-in relationship without ever having learned these skills, you are practically asking for trouble. It's hard to learn to live alone, but it's really a necessity in order to bring true maturity to a relationship.

If you have never had to deal with an overflowing toilet at three in the morning or neighbors tap dancing on bare floors in the apartment above you when you are trying to work on your income taxes, you haven't experienced the reality of living alone.

• • • • • • • •

Living alone was lonely and
hard at first. Sticking it out helped
me grow and gave me valuable
experience I need now.

What a time of year! Everywhere you turn there is another sign of summer. From the smell of hot dogs wafting over from the neighbor's grill to the children playing in the local park, summer is everywhere. Flowers bloom all over, and so does love.

Summer is a wonderful time of year to fall in love. For those who love the outdoors, there is little that will keep them indoors. Bike rides, romantic picnics, trips to the beach and to local carnivals all add to the magic of love in the summertime.

Walking hand in hand with the one we love, we can only be grateful that love happened during one of the most wonderful times of the year.

. . . .

Falling in love in the summer
is a special gift. I would like to hold
on to this feeling forever.

"I can't get over how I've been feeling. I'm really, truly relieved Bob is gone," shared Flora with her next-door neighbor. "So why do I feel so empty and strange without him around?"

Like many of us, Flora didn't understand that when something ends in our life, many of us will go through some type of grieving process. We may find it surprising that we need to grieve the very thing we want to end.

Ending a relationship that was really uncomfortable — perhaps even abusive — can still cause us to grieve. If we do not go through this natural process of loss, we carry our hurt and hidden feelings deep within us, where they are destined one day to explode. We all need to put closure on a relationship. Grieving helps us do just that.

· · · · · · · ·

I feel so exposed, as if everyone who sees me
knows why I am sad. I need to grieve
in order to help myself heal.

As youths we thought love was purely physical. After all, we thought, no one in history every felt the exact way we are feeling right now.

True adult love involves far more than just the body. True love springs from deep places within us — our hidden wellsprings — and involves our whole system and our entire life. True love is a splendid feeling. Knowing that another person feels about you the way you feel about them, that your true love would rush to your rescue in a minute or share the last piece of bread, is a warm and comfortable feeling.

Mature love moves from a physical level to a much deeper emotional level. Making a commitment to share one's whole life is not easy, but when it is made it becomes a convenant between two people in love.

• • • • • • • •

How wonderful my life feels now
that I have found the right person to
share the rest of my years.

Many people have no idea how to handle their own life, and this includes their love life.

It is only when we learn to handle our own personal problems that we can begin to be ready to manage our successes as well. Handling personal problems does not come automatically and is not necessarily a sign of maturity, since excellent business managers may have no idea how to handle problems in their personal lives.

When we learn to handle our own problems, usually by asking for help or learning by example, then we will be able to also handle our own successes. This learned, we may be ready to love again.

• • • • • • • •

The process of growing up is hard.
I thought when I turned 21 I would automatically
know everything. Now I am smart enough to
understand I will never know it all.

"I remember when I was in seventh grade," snickered Mort, "and we had this icky social studies teacher. She made us do the dumbest things, like sit up straight in the lunchroom and pay three compliments every day. We had to keep a list and turn it in. I remember when my list said, 'I told Susie her hair finally looked clean. I told Joe he wasn't looking as ugly as usual and that his sister wasn't really a midget.' It was a game, but she never caught on."

It's strange, but a task which seemed useless in childhood can become an asset in adulthood, just so we use it with wisdom. Paying a sincere compliment to another person can give both people a wonderful feeling.

This becomes especially important if we have to deal with a person we don't particularly care for.

· · · · · · · ·

The gift I give when I compliment someone is also a gift I give to myself.

The process of centering ourselves is finding out who we really are by taking the time to listen to our own needs and understand our own sensitivities, strengths and personal weaknesses.

If we really listen to our own needs, we may be surprised to find out our body knew all along what we needed. Studies have been done with both infants and dogs which show they stop eating when they are full, and they even tend to select foods that eventually balance out their diet.

It would be good if we could do the same for all facets of our lives — especially in the area of love. Love, unlike the act of centering oneself, tends to enter the heart first and the brain second.

• • • • • • • •

To stay centered I must stay aware
of what my needs are — heart,
mind, body and soul.

If we came from a family where addiction was prevalent, we learned from early childhood that our parents — the adults we knew best — were not always to be trusted. So we grew to adulthood thinking the same thing.

When we entered a committed relationship or marriage, we did so with the best of intentions, usually not even aware that we didn't fully trust other adults. This, of course, is a situation that can set up terrific conflict when one is in love.

Learning to trust is no easy endeavor. It's scary to talk over the problem and share our fears of being emotionally abandoned again, while working hard to believe the one who loves us really is committed to staying with us. Yet it is worth every moment of effort if we come out of it feeling more secure.

· · · · · · · ·

My shut-down emotions have awakened
and are growing daily with the
undying love we share.

Colin was often asked, "What do you think of this idea? What would you do to handle it?" And Colin usually had strong ideas stemming from his good business sense.

Then Colin fell in love. It didn't take long before he began to feel uncomfortable. When Hannah asked him, "Where do you want to go to eat, honey?" he always told her to decide.

Colin began to realize that outside of the business arena he was very insecure. Social situations frightened him. With the help of a therapist and his wife, Colin began to relax and feel more secure.

. . . .

As I grow emotionally, I am becoming
more well-rounded and stronger, and
I feel better about who I am and
what I am capable of doing.

Remembering her mother's words, "If it seems too good to be true, it usually is," Barb was confused. She had been dating Seth for six months now, and he was just wonderful to her.

Their relationship and commitment to each other grew, as did their mutual admiration and trust. Each time they were together felt so good, so wonderful and so warm. Yet they both moved slowly in order not to make a mistake about their feelings.

After a year of growing more deeply in love, Barb and Seth married. All their guests smiled as they watched the wedding. It was obvious that their love was true and strong.

· · · · · · · ·

It's a good thing old adages
aren't always true. Our love is wonderful
and we are a good team.

Once in a while we all do it. "I wouldn't have been issued the speeding ticket if you hadn't taken so long to get ready." Blaming is a part of human nature and we all do it occasionally.

But when the blaming gets out of hand and only one of a duo is doing all the blaming, something is out of balance and needs fixing. In fact, it can go on so far that the blamer dumps everything that's gone wrong in life on the very person they claim to be in love with.

A warning light should be blinking and a siren blaring if the person you are dating demonstrates this constant blaming behavior. Most likely this problem is deep-seated from childhood and isn't one which can be fixed very easily.

· · · · · · · ·

I will not be blamed for what
I have not done. Fortunately, I am strong
enough to leave a loved one in
order to protect myself.

Sherry was an adored only child of older parents. She could do no wrong in their eyes. In fact, Sherry was quite spoiled — anything she asked for, she got.

Because she was always forgiven any transgression, Sherry never learned to pay the natural consequences of her actions. All she had to do was pout a bit and then she would get her way again.

This attitude did not wash well when Sherry moved away from home into a sorority house at college. The sorority house had rules, and there were consequences to pay if they weren't followed. Finally, as a college student, Sherry learned what she should have learned during all the years of being lovingly parented — and she finally became a mature, well-liked and lovely young adult.

. . . .

Consequences should always be
a natural outcome of inappropriate behavior.
I am grateful to my parents for making family rules
and expecting us to keep them.

She had really had a hard life. Cara had cruel parents and a husband who abused her and the children as well. She was a good and deserving person, who in no way asked for her awful situation.

Cara divorced her husband, pulled herself up by the bootstraps and moved to Alaska. It was hard for her to be so far away from family and friends, but for the first time in her life no one was being mean to her. Over the years Cara dated a succession of men, but she had been so scarred she didn't get involved.

And then came Jordan. Never had she met a man who cherished her the way he did. Her children adored him and he them. Soon they happily and joyously married.

. . . .

*I have waited and taken good care of
my own needs and those of my family. My waiting
has paid off in the form of the best partner
I have ever known. I'm glad I waited.*

It was almost as if they had opposite pole magnets in their pockets. Fred and Dora met at work and were immediately drawn to one another. It was practically a classic "Some Enchanted Evening" rendition.

Still, both Fred and Dora were especially cautious. Having each been married one time previously, they waited to be sure they were really in love. They moved extremely carefully into their relationship, one step at a time. Regardless of how cautious they were trying to be, regardless of how long they took to decide, they fell absolutely and totally in love.

Their friends and family were so pleased. Two lovely people had found each other and fallen in love — literally across a crowded room. They stayed aware of their own needs, and their love and subsequent marriage worked out beautifully.

• • • • • • • •

Lucky is the couple who finds a true and pure love
the second time around. I pray one day
I will be one of the lucky ones too.

It was just a coffee date to begin with —
the usual "What do you do? Have you ever
been married?" and "Do you have any kids?"
type of first date. Instantly they felt quite
comfortable with each other.

Laughing as they both answered the question at once, she said, "Well, yes. I have five
children, all under ten years old." Now it
was his turn to crack up.

"I have four," he chortled, "all under eight,
and I have full custody as well."

They were so taken aback at the sheer
numbers of children that it took several
weeks to muster the courage to go out again.

When they did, both agreed to move very
slowly and cautiously, just in case they fell
in love. And fall in love they did. Two years
later, with nine children under the age of
12 as their attendants, they had a very large
wedding.

· · · · · · · ·

Take love — and life — one step at a time.
And thank God for both every day.

Bill's mother had called long distance and they were chatting. Casually she mentioned, "By the way, son, I've fallen in love. His name is Kurt and he lives in my apartment complex. I think we are going to tie the knot."

Bill was speechless. His mouth was hanging open as he stammered, "But, Ma, you've been a widow for over 30 years. You're over 70 years old, for crying out loud!"

She laughingly quieted her distraught son and made plans for them to all meet soon for dinner. Bill liked Kurt. He especially liked the way his mother was glowing all over and the way Kurt treated her with such gentle respect and obvious love.

· · · · · · · ·

Love can happen at any time of life
and create boundless joy. I hope
someday I will find love again.

They had been married for nearly 30 years and had been divorced for five. Still, every time they talked on the phone, they fell back into the same old damaging script. Bickering, ordering each other around and even doing a bit of personal prying was their norm.

Finally she realized this had to end, that their attachment was just habit and they barely had any liking for each other. They met briefly for coffee and she said, "I've been thinking this problem over. The children are gone and you really have no reason to call me at all. You may not realize it, but I can't even date freely without feeling you're looking over my shoulder. So please, don't call me — not to talk, not for anything at all except for a major family mishap. Period."

New rules established, control regained, she picked up the check and left.

· · · · · · · ·

My declaration of independence gave
me a wonderful feeling
of freedom. I deserve to be free.

This was the real thing. They both knew it. After a series of failed relationships but no marriages, Nicole and Abraham had fallen deeply and irreversibly in love.

Committed to each other and to a life together, they decided to marry.

Within a month they were fighting almost every day. If they couldn't solve their totally unspoken and sometimes unreal expectations, it was plain to see their marriage was headed for failure.

Nicole and Abe spent months with a marriage counselor, moving toward each other in understanding rather than away with unspoken expectations. Together they worked successfully to save their floundering marriage.

· · · · · · · ·

I understand the importance of talking about
our expected lifestyle before marriage to
avert potential disaster afterwards.

Alexandra was thrilled when Terry began to notice her and finally asked her out. She had had a crush on him for nearly two years, ever since they met at a ballroom dancing class.

Months passed and they became engaged. Terry's 26th birthday came and Alexandra bought him a beautiful bathrobe. Her birthday was the very next month, and she waited all day for him to give her a present or to even mention it. Alexandra told her fiance in tears, how upset she was that he had forgotten her birthday.

"I didn't mean to be thoughtless, honey," he explained. "In our house, we celebrated everyone's birthday at a huge family party twice a year. You and I can establish our own new precedent."

· · · · · · · ·

Our willingness to compromise
and our deep commitment to each other are
two of the most important components
of our marriage.

We all have a tendency to define relaxation in somewhat different terms. Jogging, a good workout at the gym, raking leaves or even baking bread are outlets for both men and women.

A problem often arises when one person construes the activities of the other as a way to ignore them. "Golf widow" is a term we have heard, as well as the term "remote-control jock."

Talking the problem over when your partner isn't involved in the actual activity is a good beginning. When we understand we are not being rejected because the one we love chooses an activity we do not like and that each of us has a right to choose on our own, we will be better off.

• • • • • • • •

*Just as we remember to leave time
for one another, we remember to talk about
our plans so no one will be hurt.*

Many a relationship has grown and been nurtured by a shared sense of humor. Being able to laugh at life's unforseen circumstances has saved many marriages.

It seems that just when tempers are ready to flare, one person can usually find the "flip-side" — the other part of the story. If both people have a good sense of humor, there is usually a good balance to the marriage.

Tamara and Art were taking a nice long shower together. One or the other kept dropping the brand-new bar of soap. Needless to say, it made the small shower smaller as that elusive bar of soap was again retrieved. Finally, in peals of laughter, they sank to the shower floor and finished scrubbing each other's backs sitting down — in fits of giggles. This wasn't such a hard situation to adapt to.

• • • • • • • •

*One never knows what a good shower
can lead to. I'm so happy I am open to learning
something new every day.*

A couple was in the grocery store at the frozen food counter. The wife said, "Oh, look, these macaroni and cheese dinners are on sale. Let's get some."

Her husband replied, "Hell, no. If you stop to figure it out, it still costs more than the stuff we make from the box."

They moved on down the aisle, picking up paper products and the rest of what they needed for their family — two adults and two small children.

Later she was pouting, so he finally asked, "What the 'heck' is wrong with you?"

"I wanted that macaroni and cheese. It's my favorite."

"Why didn't you say so?" he exploded. "I thought you were just trying to point out a sale product. Next time be specific. I'll go get some." And he did.

. . . .

When we assume the one we love
can read between the lines, we are kidding
no one but ourselves.

They came from diverse backgrounds. He was a successful dairy farmer and she was a high-power corporate lawyer. In spite of their differences, they fell in love.

One day the two were going for an evening walk. She had her walking attire on and was ready to pursue the walk at a fast trot. He was wearing sweats and wanted to stroll. "Slow down, sweetie. Take time to look at the sunset and that gorgeous river."

"Time? Who has time? I never get my work done as it is." Because he loved her so, he really tried to make it work, to ease his slow easy rhythm into hers or to have her back off a bit. Neither idea worked, and they eventually had the good sense to part ways before they got married.

. . . .

Beauty and nature do not stand still
and wait for us to find the time to admire them.
They move on each day. I try not to let the
moment pass, for I can never regain the
joy I would miss by not looking.

"Uh-uh. No way!" laughed Noel when her friend Susan wanted to fix her up with her cousin Hugh. "Forget it. I've never been on a good blind date." Sue finally got her way and the date was arranged.

Hugh turned out to be tall and handsome. He seemed to have a pleasant personality, so Noel wasn't really displeased. On their first date they went to a baseball game, a sport which they both loved, so there was little opportunity for conversation.

Their second date was more intimate, in a restaurant. Noel quickly recognized that Hugh had one major problem — he still wasn't over his recent divorce. His wife had left him for another man and he could talk of nothing else all evening. Noel pecked him on the cheek at her front door at the end of the evening and politely told him goodbye.

• • • • • • • •

It does me no good to date until
I can do so with a free mind, open and ready
to accept a new person into my life.

188

Rob was a handsome fellow who had recently broken off an affair with a woman he had loved for two years. Offers came from left and right for Rob to date, but he turned them all away.

His friends didn't understand, and finally Pete asked him what was up. Rob replied, "It's hard for me not to go out, but right now I need to respect myself and my own feelings. I'm not dating until I know I am ready to bring only me and not my memories of my old girlfriend to the date."

Waiting until the time is right shows maturity. Choosing to be alone is not an indication of failure in some people, but instead demonstrates a high level of personal courage and strong self-esteem.

• • • • • • • •

Even though it's hard to be alone,
I need time to exorcise old ghosts before
I am open to dating again.

All people are vulnerable, and certainly we all have character flaws. For this reason we each need to be understanding about the other person's sore spots.

When Tony and Anna got married, each knew and thought they understood the other. She had a bit of a temper. He tended to not do his chores as quickly as she would have liked. Both eventually learned to compromise with one another. Both were independent, but each in their own way.

When a marriage is bad, it is — to paraphrase the old nursery rhyme — very, very bad. More often, however, when a marriage is good, it's spectacular for tiny sections of time and fair the rest of the time. Accepting the truth about marriage took Tony and Anna a few years.

. . . .

Ultimately I need to depend upon myself for my own well-being. When I share my love, it will be with a person who is also independent.

Every woman Hal had ever known was dependent, weepy and unstable. Of course, every woman he had ever known was either his mother, grandmother, aunt or sister.

When Hal was ready to date seriously during his college years, he naturally expected every woman to conform with his childhood views. Each time he dated a woman who was independent, practical, intelligent and emotionally stable, he wouldn't date her again.

Finally one of Hal's fraternity buddies asked him what was going on. "I can't find a woman like the women in my family." When his friend found out what Hal was objecting to, he cracked up. It didn't take too long for Hal to wise up and understand the women in his family were not necessarily the best role models for marriage.

• • • • • • • •

Each one of us is different —
and deserves to be. No one should try to
mold another person into his
or her own image.

Our entire life is spent making decisions
— whether to buy an ice cream bar or a
candy bar, whether to take French or Latin,
whether to go to Florida or California.

When we begin to date again after a long-
term romance has broken off, we need to
make yet another decision. What are we going to tell the people we date about the one
we used to be in love with? Are we going to
be nasty? Kind? Truthful? Untruthful?

These are important decisions, for they
will tell a great deal about the type of person
we are. It's natural to some extent for people
who are dating to talk about others they
have been involved with in the past. What
they talk about may make the difference between the new relationship being wonderful
or a complete failure.

· · · · · · · ·

*Only I know my entire past
and only I can decide what I want to share.
I do not need to be unkind in order
to feel good about myself.*

The very reason most of us start to date and want to get serious is the ultimate goal of getting married and perhaps having a family. Sometimes it just doesn't work out and we find ourselves back dating again.

On occasion one person begins to feel consumed by the relationship. This loss of self, of oneness, needn't always happen. We can maintain who we are and still be in a successful relationship. By keeping the car in our own name, by keeping credit cards and bank accounts, we can maintain independence and still be deeply in love.

Two people who respect each other are not threatened when one has certain needs the other does not share. True love is living together and sharing a life. It does not necessarily mean giving up autonomy.

· · · · · · · ·

I understand it is important
that I not let myself be consumed by marriage.
I am strong enough to maintain
my own autonomy.

Every now and again we bump into a couple who obviously care very deeply about one another, but who have rightfully earned the nickname of "The Bickersons." All they ever seem to do is squabble.

Close friends find themselves uncomfortable when two people they care so much about are always at each other's throat. One day Sophia asked Gretta, "Why are the two of you always fighting? Don't you know how sad it makes us feel to see you so unhappy?"

Gretta was shocked, for neither she nor her husband had realized they were picking at each other when friends were around. They talked it over and decided to put unimportant fights "on hold" until they got home. To their amazement, most of the issues cleared up with no bickering at all.

• • • • • • • •

Fighting fairly and discussing
small problems together is one way I can
help our love to grow.

There isn't a woman among us who hasn't at one time or another been with a man who has lost his way and would rather drive an extra 50 miles than stop and ask someone for help.

The ways men and women perceive and react to the same problem are quite diverse. From chuckling at our differences and accepting them to a constant running battle and continual nagging, we each find our own way and find the person who can put up with our own foibles.

One suggestion might be to try and look at the problem through your loved one's eyes. If you are heading to a new destination, for example, buying a map might help prevent the inevitable "wrong turn" just before it occurs.

• • • • • • • •

By planning ahead and thinking about potential problems, I can prevent some of my life's "wrong turns."

Boredom overtakes us all at some time or another in our lives. With a whole weekend looming ahead, some people don't look forward to two days of boredom.

Jennifer whined to her boyfriend Steve, "We never go anywhere anymore. All you ever want to do is watch sports." Perhaps if she had instead told him, "There's a great comedian at the Rialto Saturday night, and Ed and Carole want to go. How about if we go together?" he might have surprised her with a resounding, "Fine."

Turning boredom into excitement is not an easy task and often takes careful planning. But there is no reason to be bored when there is always a wonderful potpourri of things to do on the weekend. A little conversation and advance planning can change boredom to excitement.

• • • • • • • •

Having concrete choices to offer
my friends and loved one is the solution
to my own boredom.

The very word "negotiate" conjures up the United Nations, discussion between the heads of state of major countries or union and business battles.

Rarely do we think of negotiation as a valuable learned skill for life in general and in marriage specifically. Certainly the root of our negotiating skills began in childhood. "Just one more cookie and then I'll go right to bed, okay?" The ability to negotiate may be one of the most important skills we bring with us when we fall in love and get married.

Listening to the problem, mirroring the statement and then placing it in an understandable context will usually open areas of disagreement for negotiation.

• • • • • • • •

Beginning a conversation with
"You must feel . . ." or "It sounds like . . ."
enhances my understanding and helps point
the way to successful negotiation.

Being best friends with a person we are
dating seriously and possibly even considering marrying is one of the most important
facets of any strong and lasting relationship.
Mutual admiration and respect are important, too, but they are not enough.

Having a strong mutual physical attraction is also tremendously important — more
to some, less to others. But a couple who
does not touch each other or hug and kiss
each other are missing an extremely important part of married life.

Physical attraction, whether it leads to sex
or not, is important for many reasons. It
explains why one person is attractive to us
when another is not. Add being best friends
together with a warm sex life and one has
the ingredients for a potentially wonderful
relationship.

· · · · · · · ·

*Being best friends and sharing
close physical sexual feelings are ways I can
help fan the flames of our love.*

She greeted him often in the evening with her clothes a mess and the children outside somewhere playing in the neighborhood. Clarice was a sculptor who worked at home. She and Paul were always at odds about how she lost track of time and of their children as she worked up in her attic studio.

They really needed to find a solution for this problem. The children were nearing teen years and needed more supervision than ever. And Paul didn't respect her profession at all. He always told people she "played around with clay."

One evening they went out for dinner. Both were concerned at their escalating marital problems. Really talking for the first time in years, they worked out an easy compromise.

· · · · · · · ·

Sometimes the solution is
right before my eyes and I don't see
it until I am forced to look.

It is sometimes said that the longer two people live together the more they begin to think and act alike. They often finish each other's sentences and may even dress in similar sweatsuits or other clothing.

In the older, more settled and wonderful time of life which comes at the end of one's working years, more time can be devoted to each other. Travel, which may have been a goal for years, may be possible, as well as numerous other goals which have been set aside by the need to go to work every day.

When an older couple falls in love, it infuses life into them and all the people who know and care about them. Their joy in life shines from them both as they rediscover the excitement of new love at a time of life when there is plenty of time to begin.

. . . .

My heart sings with joy as
I awaken to face each morning. I am in love
and I want the world to know
that someone loves me.

Remember high school algebra? While some loved it, many stumbled through, trying to understand how $A+B^2=X^3$. Hours spent with paper, pencils and friends who understood it better than we did helped us plow through the course. Bless those friends!

Now, when we find ourselves in conflict with the one we love, we may need to fall back to an algebraic type of conversation. "When you do A," we begin, "I feel B. But if we work together on this problem, we could become AB." For example, "When you yell, I get frightened and yell back, even though I don't want to."

By staying with the main point — the theorem if you prefer — we can work together to solve the problem, hopefully to one another's mutual benefit.

. . . .

Our love does not follow a certain formula
the way we followed algebraic formulas,
but if we work together we can solve
each problem as it arises.

Communing with nature. Some of us immediately envision camping or hiking or perhaps doing some bird watching. For others it may mean farming or gardening.

But there is one way of communing which we forget far too often. Two people who truly love each other, who are generally in sync with each other's needs, can try to remember to devote some time to just "be." To sit on the porch swing and listen to the chirp of crickets or the occasional twitter of birds is both a joy and a wonderful way to commune with nature.

Communing means being together without having the need to talk — sitting and watching the sunset for the pure joy of watching. It also means being able to share the joy life has to offer in our own personal way.

· · · · · · · ·

Those special moments of being
together are still there for us if only
we remember to take time.

So many of us remember hearing, "Silence is golden," as youngsters, but we never realized how golden until we become adults. In every situation there is a time to listen and a time to be silent — or, if we must, to be heard. While we confuse the issue a few times as we mature, eventually we learn when to talk and when to listen.

Silence is also a gift we can give to the one we love. The right to sit together without having to talk, the right to read or study alone, all these and more are gifts we can give that cost us nothing and are dearly appreciated.

· · · · · · · ·

The gold that silence can be
glows when I share silent times.

Several years ago *Ordinary People* was very popular, both as a book and a movie. However, as more and more people saw the movie, they realized there was little that was really completely ordinary about the family being portrayed.

We've come to realize that there is no such thing as a truly ordinary family anymore. There are many types of families nowadays and they seem to change composition daily — married with children, single with children, gay and lesbian parents, children being raised by grandparents and young girls having their own children.

The best we can hope for is that our lives, as we choose them will settle down to be ordinary. It seems funny to aspire to ordinariness, but a warm, stable and loving family, regardless of its composition, is what matters most.

. . . .

*I know I am ordinary, and I am grateful
for the love we give each other.*

"I can't believe these shoes were left out again! Come and get them now." Shamefaced, the teenage boy returned to retrieve his very tennis shoes. The next night he left them out again, this time at the top of the stairs. During the night his father came downstairs for some warm milk, tripped over the shoes and fell down the stairs.

As the ambulance pulled away, the 16-year-old was sobbing. "I didn't mean to hurt anyone." His mother hugged him and explained "Now you see why it is so important to put them away."

Years later when he had teenagers, he remembered how gentle and kind she had been and softened his tone before he disciplined his children. Silently he blessed his mother for her patience.

. . . .

*Sometimes the hardest lessons
to learn are the ones which hurt the most.
I can try to prevent some of
my loved one's pain.*

Attending a house of worship together, even praying together every day does not assure happiness.

Spirituality is a sharing and even joining of oneself both with others and with nature. A strong sense of religion does not imply spirituality, nor does being deeply spiritual imply one is religious.

In fact, it's a combination of the two — spirituality and religion — keeps most people feeling happy and content with their lives. To be spiritual and to share those feelings are a special gift, one which we have all been given and have only to learn to use.

• • • • • • • •

Spirituality is like a house of cards.
Each wall is a bit stronger because of the strength
of those who surround us.

Over and over Gilbert trusted other people, and over and over his trust was betrayed — first as a child and then as an adult. Even his trusty dog Fido ran away one day when he was at work and never was seen again.

Learning to trust again seemed an impossible task to Gilbert. After all, who could he trust? Not knowing where else to go, Gilbert began at a church, in a confessional. With his priest's encouragement, Gilbert joined a singles group at church and to his surprise found some friends.

From then on it got easier. With his newfound friends to guide his way and hold his hand, Gilbert became a trusted and valuable friend.

· · · · · · · ·

*I can put my broken trust
behind me as I move into new and more
trusting relationships.*

"Don't carry a chip on your shoulder," is a phrase we heard often as youngsters. "It might make people think you have a bad attitude." And so we tried hard to be "good" and never get into trouble.

Nowadays "an attitude" means anything from looking proud and cocky to what the younger crowd calls "dissing" another person — in simple English, disrespecting or talking badly about another person.

When one is in love, however, attitude has an added dimension. How we act with the person we love, whether we show respect or disrespect, how we act when times are hard or in trying circumstances often define how other people view us. Trying to keep a positive attitude, even during the more difficult times, shows we respect ourselves and the ones who surround us.

· · · · · · · ·

I try hard to be a good example
and to be positive around
other people.

208

Dr. Ruth Westheimer has moved sex from the bedroom to the tip of our tongues. Through her excellent work, she has desensitized Americans so we are no longer afraid to say out loud words like "sex," "orgasm," "penis" or "vagina."

Rather than sex being the end-all, be-all we thought it was in high school, we recognize that sex is one crucial part of an extremely intricate love relationship.

If one piece doesn't fit, the whole puzzle can't be completed. Much like the components of a good meal, time spent talking during dinner or when taking a walk, sex fits — if and when we want it to — into the pattern of our love life. Thanks to Dr. Ruth, we can more easily ask for help if the sexual part of our love doesn't fit well.

· · · · · · · ·

The sexual revolution lives!
I continually learn more about myself and
my own needs while I please
my partner.

The tickets for the concert had been purchased months before. Vicki was disappointed when Loren called to tell her he had a headache and didn't feel up to the concert. He said she should use the tickets, but she said she would rather be with him.

They had a quiet evening, eating a carry-in dinner, then playing cribbage. His headache was nagging, but not so bad that he couldn't enjoy the game. When it came time to count up the score, Vicki asked, "Who won?"

Then Loren took her hand in his and said, "Vicki, I love you and can't imagine life without you. When you said it was fine to miss the concert, I knew for sure. You are kind and loving. Vicki, will you marry me?"

With an affirmative smile from Vicki, Loren hugged her hard and proclaimed, "We both win!"

· · · · · · · ·

When the right person finally came into my life,
I didn't waste any time. Life is too short
to wait when a person is really in love.

For months they had been dating, and like many couples today they had been most cautious about having sex. The time was rapidly approaching, however. They both knew that soon they would have to make a decision.

"I have something to tell you," he whispered. "I'm not sure how to begin." Fearing the worst, she quietly waited until he spoke again. "Four years ago I had colitis so bad they had to remove part of my colon and I have an external bag to collect my stool."

Relieved, his girlfriend spoke quietly, "Is that all? Is that what has been bothering you? I fell in love with who you are, and if this is part of your life, then I will get used to it." Needless to say, that evening got quite amorous, and everything turned out fine.

· · · · · · · ·

It's hard to know when to share
a secret, but I truly trust the person I love
and know my secret will be kept.

While people are certainly not commodities, we do have a tendency to label each other. Noticing a wedding ring, for example, might make us assume someone is not available, just as no ring might let us assume the person is available to date. Labels, of course, may or may not be true.

For a long while after we have been divorced, widowed or have broken away from a lasting love, we feel emotionally unavailable for dating. "No thanks," we answer, "I'm just not ready yet. It's too soon."

Some people cling to unavailability literally for the rest of their adult lives. Others know after several months have passed that they are ready to enter the dating mainstream again. Perhaps a bit frightened, we brave it out and start to date.

• • • • • • • •

*I am frightened to begin,
but I have become stronger in these
past few months and am ready to
try to meet someone new.*

There are a lot of things we need every day — food, clothing, shelter — and our daily dose of joy, feeling loved and loving in return. Joy and love can often be found in the most unexpected places.

Without joy, life is pretty boring. Imagine, for example, what it feels like to slide into a freshly-made bed on a cold winter evening. Delicious! And think of the smell of apple cider or a fresh-cut rose. Conjure up the touch of a baby's soft smooth skin.

Love should be joy-filled. With love entering the scene from unexpected quarters, the joy nearly makes us burst with excitement. We can give joy, share joy and store joy for future memory. Joy is ours for the taking.

• • • • • • • •

Each time I experience joy
I add it to my emotional joy-bank.
I can make a withdrawal
whenever I wish.

Larger numbers of us than we can imagine grew up in homes where happiness wasn't part of daily life. In fact, it wasn't part of life at all.

Since there is no magic moment at which we become mature, we tend to measure our lives in terms of what stage we are in. Getting a good job, marrying and having children are signifiers of maturity — or at least "almost" maturity.

Before too long we understand that true maturity comes not from position and status but from personal balance and a good bit of spontaneity. Additionally, if we learn to provide ourselves with the parenting we lacked as youngsters, we can "grow ourselves up" and really get on the road to true adult maturity.

. . . .

*Age in years alone does not indicate
maturity. I see now it comes from a balance of
work and play, from loving others freely
and loving ourselves as well.*

214

Under the right circumstances most of us enjoy watching people in love just so long as their behavior is appropriate and doesn't leave us squirming.

Holding hands in the mall or on a walk is comfortable to most observers. Necking and panting over one another in the restaurant makes us feel like voyeurs and can ruin our meal as well. We often avert our heads or ask for our table to be changed, embarrassed by this inappropriate behavior.

In fact, as we date again and perhaps fall in love, we need to differentiate between sexual intimacy and intimate but appropriate behavior. Intimacy is an important facet of both friendship and love. Intimacy is a form of sharing; it implies good times spent together and warm conversations; it shows deep caring for another.

. . . .

Intimacy weaves in and out of our love relationship every day. I have enough personal control to be appropriate in public.

Walt was different from any man Gloria had ever dated. He was gentle and kind, and he dearly loved to surprise her. "Guess where we are going this evening?" he would tease, and then show her two tickets to a sold-out concert. Gloria would be delighted.

Walt was a great decision-maker, but Gloria had a real problem making decisions — a serious deficit in his eyes. At first it wasn't too bad. "Where do you want to eat?" he often asked. She would reply that she would go anywhere he wanted to go.

Walt really loved Gloria, but he got increasingly annoyed with her inability to make any kind of decision. He didn't want to live with a woman who forced him to make all the decisions. Unless she changed, Walt saw no way out but to break it off.

· · · · · · · ·

I need a certain amount of constancy
in my life, and I can make a difficult personal
choice in order to feel comfortable.

It's a big decision when two people in love decide to live together, even though recent studies show there are slightly more divorces when the couple lives together before they marry.

There are, we think, dozens of reasons to live together. From saving money to getting used to one another's personal habits, living together is often what both people choose to do. Each one may be shocked at how many items the other owns. And what do they do with two stereos, three televisions, a multitude of books and 12 boxes of assorted clothing that must be saved — just in case?

It's often better to start fresh with a new apartment so one person isn't moving into the other person's "turf." In that way both people start anew and storage space can be fairly divided.

. . . .

When I choose to live with my loved one,
it will be after our marriage.

217

Sharing is part of a committed, serious and mature relationship. Just when we carefully move into a new relationship, just as we learn each other's likes and dislikes and become used to each other's idiosyncrasies, something new pops up which makes us take a closer look at the one we love (or think we love).

Perhaps she discovers his apartment is totally messed up and even smelly — and she's a neat freak. Maybe he loves collecting fine wine and her entire upbringing disallows any drinking at all. Or maybe — and this is hardest of all — the act of making love may be completely one-sided or totally incompatible. A strong relationship needs balance. It is evident that one-sided relationships must end.

· · · · · · · ·

*Before I "write off" a person
I care deeply about, I need to be sure my
reasons are fair and that I am being
honest about our problem.*

Once in a while we hear about a couple who adopted an infant and then got pregnant within a few months. Though these pregnancies are relatively rare, we seem to hear about them every time they occur.

Another delightful story we hear happens when people in their 40s or 50s who have resigned themselves to being single all their lives meet someone — usually in the most unexpected place — and fall passionately in love. Before they even know what hit them, they are happily no longer single.

The love that comes unexpectedly, especially when we had given up hope of meeting someone special, often happens with such intensity we spin with joy. Late love might just be the very best love of all.

· · · · · · · ·

*How grateful I am that I decided
to go grocery shopping on a Saturday night
and for the love gift I have received.
I was fine alone, but I am so happy to
have the chance to share my life.*

219

One of the most important personal attributes we can have is a sense of feeling peaceful with ourselves — with who we are and what we do. People who are not peaceful are often not well-rooted and may have had serious problems in their family as children.

Through group work, personal therapy or self-help, we can learn to forgive family or friends for transgressions or improper behavior. Even those who have been sexually abused as children can learn to love themselves, to forgive and to find personal peace.

Regardless of how wronged we were as children or how unhappy we have been so far in adult life, learning to forgive and then moving on to find true personal worth and a sense of peace living within our own body is crucial to our emotional well-being.

· · · · · · · ·

My childhood was chaotic and
left me unable to love. From this day forward
I will work toward forgiveness, until
I can forgive myself as well.

When two people fall in love — really, truly in love — they generally expect to follow
a normal progression or pattern. After the
first few years, children generally come
along. And before we even know what has
happened, the children grow up and move
away. The house that was always too small
suddenly becomes too large.

Sitting together over dessert one evening
were two women three decades apart —
mother and daughter.

"What about your husband, honey? What
about the two of you? You know, if you
don't invest time and energy in your marriage now, you won't have a marriage 20
years from now. Your children will naturally leave and never turn back. You need to
have a strong union — it will just be the
two of you."

· · · · · · · ·

We must remember to put love first.
Keeping our lives love-centered
will keep our union strong.

As our adult children grow up and move away, we are faced with many decisions. At this time many women go back to school or begin for the first time. At the same time their husbands may want to wind down the amount of time they spend at their work.

In the late 40s and 50s the couple may begin to drift apart, though they hadn't meant to. Unless they consciously make time to spend together talking, regrouping, compromising and really creating a new life plan, their long marriage may not survive.

Middle-aged couples who are just now getting together may share similar problems. So much in love, yet each one wanting to live their own life, their love may end before they really begin just for lack of compromise.

• • • • • • • •

*Where there is love and willingness
to communicate and compromise, we will be able
to work out our differences and find a
lifestyle that suits us both.*

Everyone loved being around Lina and Tony. Everyone envied and emulated their marriage.

Even as they aged they still kept up all their individual interests. Tony, a retired engineer, could be found two afternoons a week helping out in a junior high school shop class and one morning a week driving for the Red Cross. Lina also loved to volunteer. She ran a quilting class for beginners.

But what they were envied for most was their unabashed joy at being together and their spontaneity, which at times bordered on the absurd. One morning Lina awoke to find Tony's nose pressed against the window. "Look! It snowed last night. Let's get dressed and make a snowman." Hand in hand they headed outdoors to play.

• • • • • • • •

I can continue having fun at any age.
Lucky is the couple who can share
their joys and sorrows and face
life with a smile.

He had been dating her for some time now and was getting to know her children better. They were eager for him to arrive for each date, for he always had some candy or gum or a little trinket for them.

After the wedding Dave adopted all three children, aged two to seven. For a while they still expected presents. Soon they realized he was really their daddy now and that presents came on birthdays and other special occasions. Instead, once a month each child got a "daddy date," where they got to choose what the two of them would do.

Dave inherited a wonderful family and Anita, who loved him dearly, respected immensely the way he had learned so quickly to be a wonderful dad.

. . . .

*Lucky is the person who seems to
have it all, for underneath they work hard
to keep their relationship and strong
parenting on an even keel.*

The ability to compromise, we are told, is the earmark of successful love. For the most part, this sage information is true.

When one person compromises too much or is the only one doing the compromising, both life and love can be too lopsided to bear. Sometimes, on more important matters, we just need to stand by our values and our morals. Even some petty little thing we just cannot give up on can cause a problem.

At other times we may be doing all the compromising for a short period of time. Then the tables suddenly turn and our partner takes our side, agrees and bends over backwards to understand our needs and our viewpoints. That there is no pattern with compromise keeps the suspense — sometimes unwelcome — in our lives.

· · · · · · · ·

I understand each day must be filled
with give and take, including compromise, and
I am ready and willing to try.

225

A very small percentage of us really feel self-assured all the time. We may look assured and confident, but even big-time executives may have holes in their socks.

Who we appear to be is not necessarily who we really are. Nearly everyone is frightened to give a speech, for example. Poll 100 people and probably 90 will list being in front of a large group as one of their biggest fears.

It's so important to know that in life, especially when we are dating again, people may look perfect, but underneath it all they are still very insecure. "I should have gone to the bathroom before I left the house" is one common thought many of us have had on the way to pick up a blind date. "How will my date look? I hope this one is halfway decent," we say, as we pull into the driveway.

• • • • • • • •

Inadequacy bothers me once in a while.
I have learned to push aside my fears, and this
has enhanced my self-esteem.

It actually was a remark overheard at a family wedding that set them all rocking with laughter. "When I was a youngster," remarked Lila, "any sex education I got was from living on the farm. By the time I was married and pregnant I finally figured out how I got that way."

"Well, that's nothing," said her daughter Julie, who was just over 40. "My generation was into free sex, Woodstock, marijuana and LSD. I didn't do much of it, but lots of people I knew did. I always wondered what free sex was like."

"If you think you're curious, what about me?" chirped Sara, who at 23 was the youngest present. "With all the sex problems around these days, the sexual revolution passed me by altogether. And I'm glad. I'm saving myself for the right man."

• • • • • • • •

Recently I have learned to be open and honest when discussing all topics with my loved one.

Respect. Most of us have been raised to show it, particularly to our elders — our teachers, our older relatives — and even to friends our own age. Showing respect not only signifies we care about another person, it shows we have enough personal respect to let ourselves show it openly.

When two people fall in love, there is much more than just respect at stake. Deep personal feelings — from how much we care about the one we love to what our life intentions are to developing a permanent relationship — shine through in all we do.

Self-respect must be strong before we can show a deep and special kind of respect to someone else. Two people who love each other deeply keep on respecting one another through good and bad times.

. . . .

*Our commitment to work at love
and always be there for one another, through
good and bad times, is the most
important respect of all.*

Remember this song, a haunting melody which applies so thoroughly when love isn't working? "It's the wrong time and the wrong place, though your face is charming it's the wrong face. It's not his face, but such a charming face, that it's all right with me."

These lyrics really said it all. Time has a tremendous amount of influence on whether we fall in love. Timing needs to be right in order for the seed of love to grow. Chance meetings, like the one in the love song, sometimes do work. A date just sort of happens and a spark ignites so strongly one would have to be there to believe it.

One should not assume an accidental love can never occur, for they do. Working on the premise that occasionally eyes do meet and interest in the other person flares immediately, a chance meeting when it might be the right person shouldn't be passed by.

· · · · · · · ·

I am open to the possibility that new love can begin in the most unexpected quarters.

When we were small, some of us pictured ourselves spending our middle-aged years sitting on a park bench like the elderly people we saw feeding the pigeons each day with scraps from their lunches.

Today bike trips, jogging through the park or working out at a health club may become as much a part of life as reading, watching television and going to the movies.

Enter instead the more active and happier middle-ager, square-dancing, bowling or playing a set of tennis. So many times people become friends and begin to date because of a newly-developed hobby or sport. The love which occurs later in life can be one of the greatest loves of all, since it comes unencumbered with all the responsibilities we carried during our younger years.

• • • • • • • •

Imagine being able to eat when I want and sleep when I choose. I move eagerly into my middle years, looking for fun and hoping to meet new friends.

Shawn was incredibly eager for the weekend to begin. It would really be exciting, but Marie just didn't know it yet. They worked hard all week and played hard all weekend, mostly with their children. They liked doing family chores together and they also enjoyed outings to the mall and going to the movies together.

On Friday morning Marie found a card from Shawn under her pillow. "Meet me at the Hotel Coronado in Chicago at 6:00 p.m. and bring a toothbrush. P.S. Drop the kids at my mom's on the way."

Shawn had completely choreographed an incredible romantic weekend. Knowing her kids were happy allowed Marie to totally relax with Shawn. The two of them had a weekend they would never forget.

· · · · · · · ·

I can take the initiative to plan
romantic times for my true love
and me to share.

Sharing confidences with friends is fine, but we all know that there are certain friends we can share anything with and others who will tell our secrets. We have found out the hard way who they are.

When we are in love and deeply involved with someone, we should not be so quick to share all our confidences, even if the person we are talking to has been a life-long friend.

Some secrets are meant to be kept between a man and woman, especially as their relationship develops. We have a new person to share certain very special moments with now, and our old friends will need to understand that there are just some aspects of our lives they should not ask about or do not have the right to know.

• • • • • • • •

The two of us have fallen in love
so thoroughly and well that we can talk about
anything without risking our love. Being
able to confide in a loved
one helps us both.

"My wife doesn't understand me. She is never there to hear what I have to say. She doesn't even respect how hard I work. It's like talking to a blank wall when I go home at night . . ." On and on he droned. And then he hit on her.

"How about you and me, toots? I'll take you out on the town tonight. We'll do it up right — huh? Whaddya say?" Arm in arm they left, both out to have a "good time." It was a sad scene to behold.

In fact, there are many couples who really don't understand one another. If they are still in love, however, then the answer isn't a beer, a barstool and a cheap date — it's a marriage and family counselor and lots of love, time, energy, caring and patience.

• • • • • • • •

Our love can be saved.
I can work hard and do my part so
we come through therapy with a sense of
renewed commitment and some new
communication skills.

What goes around always comes around, we are told. Yet we wonder how this can be true when it seems that we are always the one involved in some crisis or another.

All of us know that to have a friend one must be a friend. It's hard to recognize that being a good friend in a time of crisis — when a family member dies, when we lose a child or when a divorce occurs — really indicates our depth of caring and friendship.

It may be years before our friends need us to help them. What goes around really does eventually come around, perhaps not in equal amounts, but eventually through the years our friends need us as much as we need them. No one leads a perfect life. As we move through each crisis, we want our friends and family to be there.

• • • • • • • •

I will continue to help my friends,
even if they can't help me. When I help,
I get as much as I give.

It was advice given when we were younger, usually by an older and more experienced adult. "Go ahead, sit down and write out everything you are feeling right now — every bit of it — but don't ever mail the letter, especially if what you say might be hurtful to the other person.

"Put it, unsealed, in your desk or dresser drawer for three or four days. Then take it out and read it. If you still have the same strong feelings, go ahead and mail your letter."

Many a tragedy and potential embarrassment was averted by this sage advice of using the "drawer mailbox." How many foolish and harsh words we avoided by taking the time to think it over. A letter dropped in the box can never be called back, and the hurt feelings it may cause can last a lifetime.

. . . .

*Words written and dropped in the mailbox
too soon may haunt me forever. I will think twice
before I mail away harsh words.*

235

The circumstances surrounding the end of our first love can be so emotionally devastating that we vow never to fall in love again — to live the rest of our lives solo so we won't ever be hurt again.

Being in love was wonderful. But then a tragedy occurred, such as being widowed by a drunk driver, losing a loved one to a heart attack or terminal illness or having the person we loved so dearly decide they just didn't love us anymore and leave. We may come out of that love so bruised and battered emotionally that we are unwilling to let ourselves love again.

Many of us, in spite of what we were planning, fall in love regardless. From 19 to 90, life once again can become joyful and full of surprises as we share the years with our new love.

• • • • • • • •

While my mind knows that I never want to
lay myself open and be vulnerable to loving again,
my heart is sending me different messages.

Pete and Susie were high school sweethearts for three years, and then Susie was ready to leave for college. When she said goodbye to Pete, he threatened to commit suicide. His reaction was a form of emotional blackmail not at all true love.

At the end of her second year of college Susie met David in chemistry class. They were so totally compatible that they even thought alike. Two wonderful years of getting to know each other led to planning their wedding.

A summer garden wedding, complete with tent, a string quartet and a glowing bride and groom, taught Susie that she was right to break up with Pete. True love lasts, feels wonderful and gives both people an equal sense of joy and astonishment.

· · · · · · · ·

Love means waiting.
Waiting for the right person, for
the right time and finally the time
comes to share our life.

237

If two people who are both in top management positions fall in love, there is going
to be competition between them, sometimes
subtle, often more overt. Without recognizing it, they may be so much alike that they
constantly struggle for superiority.

Managing another person's life never
works. How much they are really in love
and how committed they are to one another
is what may eventually send the couple to
seek marriage counseling.

Learning to compromise and putting our
loved one's needs ahead of our own demon-
strate willingness to learn and change. Working at their love constantly, a couple learns
about marriage and subsequently about life
as well.

· · · · · · · ·

Marriage shouldn't be considered
a business proposition. The special joy
that comes from knowing I can share my
life with someone who loves me
back is awesome.

His beloved wife had died suddenly of leukemia, leaving him with an infant. After a year or so he began to attend Parents Without Partners. There were other single people there, some with small children like his.

It was apparent that almost everyone there wanted to get married. Their losses had turned their lives upside-down like his. But it was a good group for him. He gained back emotional equilibrium and his desire to date once again.

Occasionally he dated, but it took two years to find Janet. Their circumstances had been remarkably similar, except Janet's husband had died of a brain tumor. Their children liked each other, which was a good thing, for they were soon to become a family.

· · · · · · · ·

What joy I face as I awaken
each morning with my beloved at my side.
I thank God for giving me a
second chance to love.

Wanda and Larry, always next-door neighbors, had fallen in love and were engaged. The neighborhood was buzzing with the happy news.

Weeks before the wedding, Wanda was in a horrendous automobile accident. Rushing to her bedside, Larry was terrified she wouldn't live. She did live, but became a paraplegic. "You've been wonderful, but I don't expect you to marry me now — not the way I am."

"You are the woman I love. I want to share my life with you. If you will still have me, I want to be your husband. I know our life will be completely different than what we planned, but we can make it together if we work to keep our love and mutual respect alive."

. . . .

*Love based only on looks is
a shallow type of love. Looking deep within,
I can find inner strength and love
deeper than I could imagine.*

Something just didn't feel right. Tom and Sharon had been dating for six months and were moving into a more intimate romance. They enjoyed being together immensely.

Tom couldn't figure out why, but as they became closer she seemed to depend upon him just a bit more than before. Her frequent phone calls held a slight sense of desperation, especially late at night. He became more and more uncomfortable. In fact, he felt so weird about what was happening that he decided to stop dating her.

He met her for coffee one Sunday morning and told Sharon face to face. She became hysterical and left, screaming. Later she called to tell Tom that life without him would be worthless. He finally understood that she was, unfortunately, mentally ill. Tom said goodbye and hung up the phone.

· · · · · · · ·

I am grateful I let my head overrule
my heart, for I may have saved myself from
a very difficult relationship.

In summer people go to the beach for many reasons. Some swim or picnic with family or friends. Others go to soak up the sun and enjoy a carefree day away from home.

Week after week these activities go on. A bit of Frisbee, a little volleyball and eventually some new relationships grow. If this type of lifestyle works, it's a nice easy way to make new friends, both male and female. Evening parties happen with no previous planning. Ah, yes. The beach is often a very special place to meet new friends.

· · · · · · · ·

"To the beach," I say.
Many lonely people like me will be
there too, and I am ready for
special new friendships.

A man and woman work in the same office, and after a while they begin to talk. Realizing they have an awful lot in common, they may go out for lunch one day. Then they start meeting for coffee and finally actually make a date to go to a fine restaurant for dinner. A common scenario, right?

But now what happens? Assuming both people have jobs they like, what would happen if they really fell for each other? Many offices have special policies against office dating, so then it has to be done on the sly so no one will know. Someone always manages to "spill the beans."

When love gets to the point of no return, when we are sure, then a serious discussion about the repercussions of our actions is necessary. Mature adults will find a way to solve their problems.

· · · · · · · ·

Since we are deeply in love, together we can work out ways to meet both our needs in our careers and our relationship.

243

No two people on this earth are exactly the same. Even identical twins quickly find their own path of individuality as they mature, just as the rest of us do.

People who are in love often have differences in personality which make it nearly impossible to live together. While some people might tolerate every personal habit from fingernail-chewing to smoking, others might find those behaviors disgusting and say so. Factor annoying habits in with basic differences in people, in family expectations and religion and one has the potential for disaster.

Chemistry is often the first thing which draws two people together. Mutual hobbies, good communication skills, compatible families and unqualified love help keep them together.

· · · · · · · ·

*Each day I will honor our differences
and polish my listening skills.*

Not surprisingly, greater numbers of people are volunteering these days. From helping in soup kitchens to delivering food for Meals on Wheels to teaching kids algebra, volunteerism is definitely on the rise.

It's a largely unexplained phenomenon since the middle class stays middle class, yet pays more and more income tax. With less money in our collective pockets, we still find the time to reach out, both individually and as a nation, to help people in need.

Canvassing neighborhoods together all summer for a non-profit organization offering information about acid rain, Krissy and Jules became good friends and fell in love. Lots of wonderful people volunteered to come to their wedding.

．．．．．．．．

If I should happen to meet someone
special while doing volunteer
work, that would be lovely.

Michael came from a very proper family — one which believed emotions were taboo. Manners and neatness were everything to his family. As a small boy he used to dream about eating a dripping ice cream cone outdoors and letting it stain his shirt in public.

Michael's emotions and actions were completely repressed. He never showed anger. When he went to college, he fell in love with Kristen. After graduation they married and in the course of a few years had two children.

One afternoon Michael's temper exploded. It blew until he began to sob with shame and embarrassment. Michael was hospitalized, but Kristen stayed with him and helped him get into personal and group therapy once he was home. He did get better.

· · · · · · · ·

Through the work I am doing with my support group and with the wonderful help of my friends, I now understand that to be whole I must be allowed to show my emotions.

Jeremiah's mother had asked Katie to meet her privately and not to tell her son. "Katie," she said, "please don't marry my son."

"It was probably one of the strangest lunches I've ever had," shared Katie. "At first I thought his mother was a selfish woman who didn't want her only child to get married. I know now I was wrong. She asked me if Jer had told me he had been married before, had a child and frequently beat his wife. Then she said he had spent two years in jail. At first I was stunned and not sure she was telling me the truth, so I hired a detective who checked and told me it was all true."

It was over between Katie and her fiance. Jeremiah's mother was a courageous woman who set aside her own feelings to keep a lovely woman from becoming her son's next victim.

• • • • • • • •

It was over between us as soon as I found out he was an abusive person. I am a good person and no one has the right to hit me.

They met at a ballroom on an "open danc-ing" night for people over 60. They danced the night away and greeted the sun over cof-fee and doughnuts. Sydney and George danced together for the first time as if they were meant to be dance partners forever.

"I haven't had such an evening in 20 years," she gushed. "I hope we can do this again." Syd practically floated home. What she didn't yet realize was that George was floating too. He called her within moments of arriving at home.

Besides loving to dance and doing it often, George began to court Syd in a wonderful old-fashioned way. She laughed as she spoke long-distance to her daughter, "He loves the same old songs I love. He even sings them to me while we dance. Life is so wonderful!"

• • • • • • • •

When it comes to love, my mind is open.
As I go to new places, I am bound to find
my dance partner somewhere.

Just when it seems we are so overloaded that we cannot take anymore, something we never dreamed would happen to us, happens — the person we have loved for so long is leaving us.

We feel certain we will never get over this horrible shock, this feeling of being dumped, but eventually we start toward recovery.

Separated long enough to go out with friends, we start to regain our social footing once again and take a chance on a real date. The first one is hardest, since we find ourselves talking too much about broken hearts. Before too long the old love becomes part of the past and we begin to develop new relationships again.

· · · · · · · ·

The doors are open. I am strong now and
ready to walk through them.

There comes a certain time after our past love has dissolved when we realize it's really, really over. We no longer wait for the phone to ring or the card of apology to come in the mail. We stop mulling over past affairs and problems.

When the time is right, we know it. Time to step out, to move foward, to spend time with old friends and make some new ones. Energy might very well come to a peak. It's time, perhaps, for a new job, maybe even in a different city. It's time for a wonderful new life. Each of us, as we know, has short-term bursts of energy when we know it's the right time.

Don't delay. The magic moment of readiness may pass by, our energy level may slack off and all the opportunities that might have presented themselves may never appear.

· · · · · · · ·

My life isn't defined just by my past.
I have a whole new future ahead of me,
and I am ready to begin.

Every person defines thrift in a different way. What is thrifty to one may be out-and-out luxurious to another.

When two people fall in love, more than just love factors into their relationship. Religion, lifestyle and family matters all play a part in a relationship. There are certain qualities and behaviors to watch for. Does your loved one tell you what to do and how to do it? Is money an issue which always generates a fight?

There is a big difference between being thrifty and being a tightwad. One can learn to be thrifty and feel good about saving money. However, if someone is trying to control every penny you spend and holds on to their own money like a fly on flypaper, perhaps the relationship needs to be reconsidered.

· · · · · · · ·

I don't have to marry a person, no matter how much they love me, if I am made uncomfortable about any aspect of life.

If it seems too hard to make great strides after your love has ended — for any reason at all — then it is a good idea to learn to take baby steps again, steps toward a brand new life.

The first step is to step out, literally. Lunch with old friends or colleagues, a movie with an acquaintance or shopping with a relative is a good way to start. Tell all the people you are close to what has happened. It's fine to ask for sympathy, and those are the very people who might eventually introduce you to a friend you may date some day.

Go to singles events with other singles to see what it feels like to be available again. Eventually you will be able to work into a real date, one on one, with a person you have met.

. . . .

No one runs a marathon before they practice
running for months and months.
I am practicing for my new life.

Finding the right time to work on hard relationship problems is not easy. Both people need to be receptive to have a serious discussion. This is especially difficult when one person wants to "talk" and the other person wants to "think."

Conflict is hard to deal with when two people live together — let alone two who are trying to keep a somewhat shaky relationship on an even keel. There is something about the phrase, "We have to talk," that puts us off.

During the time before "the talk" we are thinking — what can we say, how will we say it? Telling someone we really love that it's over, that there are too many differences, that there are too many fights, is one of the most difficult "talks" we ever will have.

• • • • • • • •

Before I say something I will regret, I give myself a "cooling off" period. I need to look truthfully at our relationship and then decide what is best for me.

253

While opposites do attract, relationships are usually more successful if a great deal is shared in common. Individual likes and dislikes are fine, but certain basic life aspects should be mutually shared.

Basic things like respect for each other and our family members, having the same religion, attitudes about family life and raising children all work better if they are held in common.

Those important aspects which are not held in common should be respected by one another. One may love boating, another may hate the water. If what we have in common and what we do separately are equally respected, we can fully enjoy time spent together and share those things which we hold in common.

. . . .

To find a certain comfort level I need to be able to share most aspects of my life. Finally I care enough about myself to take care of my own needs.

Settling down after months of uncertainty, Dennis was finally feeling comfortable about being divorced. He loved his job, loved coming home each evening and taking his two greyhounds jogging. After dinner, he then looked forward to a sound night's sleep — until Corrine moved in next door.

He tried hard to ignore his pretty new neighbor, but she was so sweet and nice that his resolve not to date eventually broke down. He finally decided to ask her out for dinner.

By their third date Dennis was arguing with himself, "I don't need a girlfriend. I'm just fine alone." But there was just no way to avoid his feelings about this wonderful next-door neighbor. Every time he thought of her smile, he would catch himself grinning.

· · · · · · · ·

*I thought I liked being alone, but I understand
now that what I really needed
was some time to be ready to love again.*

One of the worst feelings anyone can have is someone giving them an ultimatum. "Pay this overdue bill in ten days or we cut off your gas," though, is a direct consequence of not paying the bill.

But when a person we love gives us an ultimatum, it feels like an affront, a slap in the face. "Lose 20 pounds before the wedding or there will be no wedding!" If that person doesn't love us as we are, for who we are, then they better realize that the first ultimatum will be just one of an endless series.

Ultimatums are threatening and may even make us do exactly the opposite. Control should not be an issue in a relationship. The issue instead should be equality.

· · · · · · · · ·

No one is going to control my actions but me.
I have worked hard to feel proud
of myself and will not let my self-pride go now.

Too often people who have physical impairments are seen as asexual and different. Some people have a difficult time understanding that a person with cerebral palsy or one who is visually impaired has the same needs and desires as anyone else.

This group of people may or may not have trouble finding people to date. Many people with handicaps date in the mainstream, get married, have children and live full lives.

There are special groups designed to introduce people with handicaps to each other, should they want to use those services. People who have handicaps are just like everyone else. Most people want a happy life, living it the way they choose with the person they love.

· · · · · · · ·

By looking past a handicap to find the person
within, I may just find one of
the most loving and special people of all.

Social masks. We all hide behind them at one time or another. Shake hands, act sincere — and behind the mask we may be feeling bored or even seething with anger. Some people never let down their guard, never let people in to see their secret or private self, never take off the mask.

While hidden behind their masks, people behave in ways that may surprise us. During accidental "mask slippage" we may see sadness or a look of total deceit.

Staying hidden behind social masks obviously serves some people well, as they are very robotic in all their business and social contacts — proper, but robotic. Maybe they are using the mask to hide a deep fear of socialization or intimacy.

· · · · · · · ·

If I need to use a social mask for now,
I hope I can soon take it off
and find myself smiling underneath.

Supposedly our human ability to keep hope alive, even in the worst of circumstances, is one reason we have continued to develop on the evolutionary ladder. The other reason, of course, is that humans cry. Too often hope and tears hold hands as we try to regroup our lives in order to love again.

Humans seem to have a tendency to bounce back — even when we have reached our very lowest ebb of life. Regardless of how many times we get beaten, how many times we have dated or even married unsuccessfully, we still get a haircut, dress ourselves up and go out again — hoping this person will be the right one, hoping the chemistry, the intellect and our interest will all mesh and we will once again find love.

· · · · · · · ·

Keeping hope alive comes as second nature for me.
I always expect to bump into that
very special person or opportunity as I turn
each corner of life.

Eileen and Richard had known each other casually for years since they both worked in the same building. All of a sudden they were both single. They stopped at a local bar for a quick drink after work one evening and talked to each other for hours.

Quite by accident Eileen's hand touched Richard's leg. She apologized and smiled, and he gently touched her hand. That touch positively electrified them both. They left and stopped out front to give each other a warm, sensual and promising kiss. Just one.

From this touching experience two work friends were drawn to each other in an explosive manner. After the evening's "heat" cooled down somewhat, both realized that they had to stop, slow down and take each step slowly if they were going to pursue any kind of serious relationship.

· · · · · · · ·

"Touching experiences" can happen to anyone.
I have enough control to slow down the process so
we can date as if we've just met.

In general it's wise to trust our own instinct. Most of us were told in school, "Trust your first instinct on a multiple choice test. It will almost always be the right one." And of course when we got our tests back we lamented that we hadn't done just that.

People can have instinctive feelings about one another as well. When it comes to falling in love, a familiar look or feeling can cause a special type of chemistry, which we don't really understand but quickly learn to like. But it's definitely instinct which tells us to "go with it." We know intuitively when it feels right to keep dating and also know if we are being rushed or are ready for commitment.

· · · · · · · ·

Trusting my instinct rather than questioning it
helps me feel I am making good decisions.

We all understand being dedicated to our job, and we certainly are aware of workaholics. These people carry work to such an extreme that they can't even back off over the weekend. They bring their work home or create extra work to do over the weekend.

It may really be time to regroup if you are a workaholic or are dating one — time to look at your entire lifestyle. Is this how you really want your whole life to be? Plan ahead and delegate jobs so you don't have to bring work home.

Make sure friends know how hard you are trying to change, that you really want a social life. Be careful not to get compulsive about making this monumental lifestyle change. Compulsive living is only enjoyable to the person who is compulsive.

. . . .

As I loosen up and enjoy life, I can become less compulsive about work.

Some parents praise their child only if that child has measured up to the parents' needs and expectations. This happens to the exclusion of any of the child's needs.

This type of behavior borders on narcissism on the parents' part and is very damaging to the child. As adults, we find we do things for others all the time because our self-esteem is very weak due to our childhood need to be constantly praised.

A person who is overly self-concerned often dates one who has had less schooling or is from a lower socioeconomic class. They don't take criticism well at all, yet are especially eager to please their bosses, their friends and their loved ones.

• • • • • • • •

Run, don't walk, from this type of person and this type of abnormal relationship. A person who cannot commit to love rarely commits to anything.

Mature people will look at a problem from all angles before making a decision. They seek out a great deal of information rather than trusting anyone else to get the facts.

When it comes to making love decisions, the same strong people look at love from all aspects just as they did for business. Before they let it become an affair of the heart, they usually need to be sure the person they love is practical, mature and decisive.

Trying to look past the yanking of the "heart," the strong decision-maker works on leaving emotions totally out of the equations. Love doesn't count here, they figure. Then if the relationship doesn't work, they can't blame themselves — it was just like making a bad business deal.

· · · · · · · ·

By never opening myself up to the hurt that may come with love, I am keeping myself from ever knowing the true joy of love.

264

When some people start to feel too happy they get frightened. They are afraid if they feel totally joyful, something will happen, as it has seemed to in the past, to take that happiness away.

Instead of showing true love, the person might instead get far too "clingy," afraid that if they let go, the one they love will run away. Of course that very clinginess is reason enough to leave, and most often the one being held so tightly does eventually pull away.

Additionally, people who feel undeserving of joy have a tremendous fear of getting involved in a fight, so they never really face up to their own real problems. Like the partner who continually sabotages their loved one's diet, people who are afraid of joy may be sabotaging their own chances without even knowing it.

· · · · · · · ·

I have worked hard to learn to love myself
and I am no longer afraid
of being hurt or of feeling love and joy.

In recent divorce studies the very children we thought would be most affected and have unhappy marriages did much better than anticipated.

Because these adult children came from dysfunctional families, they often became the strongest family members. Large numbers of women come out of bad childhoods still remarkably resilient.

If this person was a good student, moderately religious and able to develop interests outside the home, they often had strong reasons to leave home when they were old enough. They were secure even though divorce had occurred in their family. These strong people of divorced parents have surprised us all and have gone on to develop their own lasting marriages.

· · · · · · · ·

Internal resilience develops at a young age.
My resilience has helped me recover from lost loves
and has helped make me ready to love again.

A lot of us walking around never learned how to express anger appropriately. Some hide it altogether, while others don't place their anger where it belongs or act inappropriately.

"Damn truck driver! He cut me off!" yelled Dirk. He knew his driving was erratic and that he had a tendency to speed — he had the check stubs to prove it. Yet Dirk never realized it was usually his fault.

When that type of temper is directed at us, it can be just awful. Even if we don't get hit, each time our loved one yells we are cut to the quick. After all, if we are in love with a person who has a foul temper, we try to pretend it doesn't hurt.

· · · · · · · ·

Overlooking anger, even when it is not directed at me, lessens my feelings of self-esteem. No one has the right to yell at me.

Two men were sitting together in a restaurant having a very serious talk. One had tears in his eyes. "I still love her, Shel. I just can't believe she left me like that. And for another guy. What do I do now?"

Still confused at Beth's actions, his friend said, "There's nothing you can do, fella. After the divorce you'll move on, kiddo. That's what you'll do."

As if in a strategic planning session, they talked about how to begin again, where he should start. "You could try that writer's group you were always talking about."

"I guess I'm not ready to try yet. I need to wait a while until I even think of dating again. I guess what I have to do now is heal and give myself the time I need to adjust."

• • • • • • • •

Time to heal is precious and absolutely necessary.
Trying to date too soon would
hurt me, and I am too fragile right now.

It was the kitty that finally did it. Funny how things happen in life. After three years of a very dry spell of dating, Pam wandered into a pet shop to look at the kittens.

Holding a beautiful Persian kitty was a good-looking man about 40. They started talking, so easily, so comfortably. He bought one of the litter; she bought another. Naturally they exchanged phone numbers to keep in touch — in order to talk about the cats, of course.

In the most unexpected place possible Pam met a new friend. We all know the end of the story. They dated a while, at least until their kittens were cats. Then they decided to get married. They had so much in common already, and besides, they were in warm, wonderful and glorious love.

• • • • • • • •

Once I stopped looking I almost stumbled over
my future spouse. I need to always
be open to new possibilities.

Jamie dated a lot, but he was never serious with any woman. As soon as the relationship got to a certain point he backed away and eventually broke contact altogether. Again and again he repeated this behavior — until he met Marta. She was so special that even he couldn't back off. Moving forward just a small bit, he let himself become more involved than ever in someone else's life. Then he stalled again.

Finally Marta laid it on the line. "Are we serious or not? What is your problem?" Jamie explained how his former wife had taken him to the cleaners financially, and how hurt and broke he was. Marta understood, but explained that she had a full-time job and expected to continue working at her executive position, and if he wanted to keep dating her she would really enjoy it.

• • • • • • • •

Honesty and openness reap their own rewards.
Talking together and gaining more understanding
and trust let us make a decision to marry.

"Second time around?" she laughed. "I'm on number three! The first two died on me after 15 and 23 years. I miss them both terribly, but I'm looking now for number three. All I have to do is go cowboy dancing and a whole flock of the 'oldies but goodies' come around."

Harriet was obviously determined to marry again. She was a buoyant older woman, full of life and always on the go.

It was apparent that it wouldn't be very long until her rope snared a cowboy to bring on home. She was vital, warm and lovely. There were many men soon contending for her attention and ultimately for her hand.

· · · · · · · ·

Some people seem to draw dates and mates like
flies. I am working hard to emulate them and
then develop my own unique style.

271

Usually it's the small children who are hurt and confused. After their mommy or daddy leaves, the other parent often brings home, over a period of months or years, people whom they are dating.

The children are often just becoming firmly attached when that person disappears and another one appears instead. Small children don't understand the concept of dating and looking for someone to marry. All they know is that someone they loved and trusted has disappeared — again.

If we need to bring home dates, then perhaps we should be more protective for our children's sake. Dating outside the home might be easier until a relationship is quite serious.

· · · · · · · ·

As I continue to date, I must remain conscious
of how it appears to my small children.
Their welfare always comes first.

"On the bus!" she shrieked. "Can you believe I've been riding on his bus for six
months and that we work only two buildings
apart? Can you imagine?"

So goes life. Just when we feel lost, we
are somehow found. Just when we feel lonely, a new friend appears. First a bus friend,
then a true friend.

Rather than spending huge amounts of
time looking all over for people to date, sometimes just living our normal lives and spending the time to look at those who always
surround us might give us a much larger
number of people to date.

· · · · · · · ·

Now I understand I was working too hard to
"catch" love. People aren't for trapping.
Instead, they are for living — and loving.

Every one of us knows at least one person who has dated someone who seemed so right for them, so kind and warm and lovely, that we were shocked as our friend picked apart the very person we perceived as so terrific.

This can happen to the same person again and again. We become distressed as they let seemingly special people slip through their fingers.

Astounded, we used to query, "But what was wrong that made you break up?" And we are told the above reasons are the reasons — nothing more. We learn after a while to keep our mouths shut, for it is apparent by now that our friends do not want to be married and are looking for a person who does not exist.

. . . .

I cannot keep looking for the perfect mate.
I understand now that I need professional
help, since it is finally obvious
I have made serious errors.

There is almost nothing worse when we are dating again, than to have part of our dating successes and failures worked through a "post-mortem" by our family members.

The morning after a date the phone rings bright and early, often with our mother on the other line, sometimes with a sister or brother. "Well? So how was it? Does this one have possibilities? Should I order any wedding invitations yet?"

This type of conversation is so discomforting and frustrating, not to speak of prying, that some people won't enter into it anymore. "Ma, leave me alone! If there is something to tell, I'll let you know. So stop driving me crazy. This is my life."

. . . .

Though their intentions are good, my anger grows as they place more stress upon an already difficult time of life. I will have to tell my friends and family their behavior is unacceptable to me.

275

For three years Matt had protected himself by not dating at all. His divorce had hit him so hard that he had seen a psychologist just to begin to function socially. After all, when one is divorced with hardly any warning, confusion and disappointment can reign.

The first time he agreed to go on a date, with a woman who worked in another department in his company, he nearly called and canceled due to his stomachache. Reluctantly he went to the play they had decided to see.

The play was nice and the woman seemed pleasant. Afterward they stopped for a light bite and coffee. She confided, "I felt so nervous tonight, Matt. This is the first time I have gone out in two years, since my husband died. It feels weird to be on a date again."

· · · · · · · ·

Regardless of how calm the other person seems,
they are likely experiencing some of the
same anxieties we are. Knowing that makes it
a bit easier to begin again.

She was going on a date tonight and for the first time, she must leave her ten-month-old daughter with a babysitter. The combination created a level of fear and anticipation that Georgia could barely stand.

When Randy picked her up, she was nervous. They had a reservation at a nice restaurant. On the way they began to talk. "I don't know if the baby will be all right. What if she wakes up and gets frightened?"

Randy suggested that since she was so nervous, they change plans entirely, and she was relieved. They stopped and rented a movie, bought some take-out fried chicken and went back to her house. They watched the movie and ate, talking comfortably all evening. He had been fun to be with and very understanding.

· · · · · · · ·

I am learning that there are
some things I must still do in small steps.

This time it was her Aunt Hermina whose friend Dora had a grandson who was coming in from New York for the week. He was a stockbroker and just too good not to go out with at least once.

"I won't do it, Mom. I'm tired of being fixed up. I feel like some poor waif who can't get a date on her own." However, her mother's sister prevailed and in a few days the stockbroker was at her apartment door. He was tall and very handsome, which cast a different light on things.

So she went, and while she didn't have the time of her life, she had to admit he was nice, polite and certainly handsome. So she accepted another date with him that week and then a third. Only time would tell if they would permanently click, but she decided that fix-ups were all right under certain situations.

. . . .

I can't let my stubbornness keep me from going out with a person who might be very nice.

Alexa felt she was stuck. She was without a boyfriend and four months pregnant. The baby's father was gone — he wanted nothing to do with them.

Alexa didn't want to date right now. So she spent a lot of time with her old friends and housemates from school. They were wonderful to her — a strong support group.

One day Jeff showed up and asked if they could talk. He explained that for years he had cared for her in more than a friendly way, but that he wasn't willing to break "house rules" when they lived together. He offered to marry her and adopt the baby with such sincerity that she began to cry. His loving offer would take time to consider but suddenly she didn't feel so alone after all.

. . . .

In the future, I will make
my decisions based on many factors,
not just my need to have someone to love.

It's the strangest thing, but each person has a personal boundary, a certain space which is theirs. If someone enters their personal space that person will most likely back away.

Most of us will not tolerate having our personal space violated and we give out very open messages. Backing away, walking away, turning around, sitting down or standing up are all clues to back off about eighteen inches.

These eighteen inches are very important when we are dating. Occasionally folks can't figure out why no one will go out with them, yet the fact that they may never even get a "yes" depends largely on how they present themselves in the first place.

· · · · · · · ·

People who feel invasive to me are those who stand
too close and encroach on my space. Finally
I have learned to say so, and most people
graciously back away a bit.

As we re-enter that ever-swelling group of people who are already dating, some of us do so with preconceived ideas of the type of person we are looking for.

For instance, when Mike heard his prospective date had been divorced and was still an active alcoholic, he canceled their date. He had gone that route once and it led to divorce. Not every person we go out with is exactly who we were dreaming about, but almost everyone has some endearing qualities.

Sometimes we just have to wait for a while to find those qualities. A man might not be willing to show tenderness until he knows a woman well, or she might feel hesitant to have him for a home-cooked meal until she is comfortable being alone in the house with him.

· · · · · · · ·

No one shows all the aspects of their personality at once. I am willing to wait for several tries to see if the person I am dating is worth waiting for.

George couldn't stand nail-chewing, yet there Deb sat gnawing away on her nails. Meanwhile, Deb was going nuts listening to George loudly chew popcorn with his mouth open.

Later, they stopped for pizza and she realized she really enjoyed being with him. So Deb took a chance and out came the words, "I have never heard anyone eat popcorn as loudly as you. Did you know you do that?" He didn't, and thanked her sincerely for telling him.

So Greg tried it out too. "As long as we are being honest, nail-biting is one of the things that drive me nuts. Do you always do that?" She broke out laughing and told him she never did, but that she was so excited about the date that she had eaten away her carefully grown nails.

· · · · · · · ·

It's amazing what we discover when we take a chance on a person we care about.

Sherry had a cold the first time they went out. She sniffled through dinner and bowling afterwards, apologizing all the while to Paul for her sniffles. He didn't kiss her goodnight, but he did ask her out again. She was fun to be with and they had fun together.

Next time it was her back. She had pulled it somehow and needed help even getting out of the car, but it had never occurred to her to cancel her date. He was amazed at the number of pain pills she took that evening.

The third time is often the charm, so he gave it one more try. This time it was her arm and her shoulder and her back. He was polite, ended the date rather early and thought, "She seems addicted to being sick."

• • • • • • • •

I don't need to get involved with a person who already has so many problems.
I must take care of my own needs first.

It does happen once in a while that two people meet and click emotionally, physically and intellectually. Before the first date is even over they are each thinking the other is too good to be true.

As they continue to date, however, they realize that they really are that rare match made in heaven. For that very reason they often go a bit more slowly, using caution before they commit themselves for life. So they spend months getting to know each other and falling more and more deeply in love.

It does happen. There is such a thing as the perfect match. It's what we all pray for, but a rare few are lucky enough to ever know.

• • • • • • • •

A perfect match in the beginning will often not last
unless both people are committed to a lifetime
of talking, of loving, of working together to solve
their problems. Then their match is truly perfect.

It's one of those weird problems many people who are dating have but few know how to talk about. What happens after the first few dates if both people really get along?

Some are terribly frightened of moving into the next stage, which might involve more physical or emotional intimacy, or both. They might have secrets they are not willing to share, or they may not be ready to make love.

So it stops right there. What had the potential of being a special relationship ends because of fear — fear of the future, fear of commitment, fear of being intimate and possibly even fear of having to share oneself with another for life.

. . . .

Being willing to move to the next stage indicates
maturity and readiness for a relationship.
It also indicates I have worked out my personal
problems that have kept me frozen in the past.

We used to hear the term "Mama's Boy" all the time, but somehow it doesn't seem to come up as much as it used to. Rest assured that there are still plenty of them around and we may accidentally stumble upon one.

There are also "Mama's Girls." Sometimes, because mothers won't allow their children to become adults, they nag and insist on knowing every detail of the adult child's life. Many adult children comply — enjoying the special care and devotion they get from their mother.

Some solve their problem by moving away because they are frustrated and want to live their own lives.

. . . .

Be aware that going home for a visit may cause past problems to resurface. For most, habits are deeply ingrained and nearly impossible to break.

It was simple enough, a barbecue invitation, complete with some old friends and one new one intended to be a blind date for Sandra.

Certainly it seemed a comfortable enough invitation, for an outdoor party with other people around, so Sandra said she would go. Actually, she was pleased to find that Ralph was rather good-looking and taller than her height of 5'10".

However, everytime Ralph found a wall or tree he would back her into it, pressing his body against hers and trying to kiss and maul her. It was a scary game of hide and seek — one that was frightening and kept Sandy from wanting to ever see this jerk again.

· · · · · · · ·

There is just no way to judge a book by its cover or a person by their looks. I can still date but carefully protect myself from harm.

Sulynn was at a strange precipice in her relationship with regard to safety. She was dating a really nice man who liked her and was good to her children.

Sulynn had no car but he did, an old one with no seat belts at all. He was more than happy to take them wherever they wanted to go. One day she sat him down and said how uncomfortable she felt that she and her children were not in seat belts and offered to help pay for them.

He laughed loud and long. "I won't have any government dictating to me what I have to do in my car. I won't wear seat belts and won't let you put them in my car." It was sad, for aside from his stubbornness about this one topic he was very special. She sadly told him they would no longer be dating.

. . . .

I will never compromise my children's or my
own safety just to stay in a relationship.
I value our lives too much to compromise.

Margie told him from the start she was afraid of water, that she knew how to swim but avoided boats and deep water like the plague. There was just one major problem — Casey spent most of the summer sailing or fishing on his boats.

Margie was upset, but Casey was not willing to let go of Margie so easily. Except for her fear of water, she was nothing short of terrific. So they sat down one evening and compromised.

"If I am very gentle and patient and we stay in shallow water and don't go fast at all when we fish, will you agree to go along? You'll wear a life vest the whole time." Eventually, Casey won Margie's trust with his thoughtfulness and patience and the next summer they enjoyed fishing and sailing together.

. . . .

Trust must be complete, and with time I can learn to trust the one I love.

Jimmy had been a widower for three years now. Finally his children were all in school the whole day. During the years since his wife had died he had really worked hard to be both mother and father, and all his children seem well-adjusted and happy.

So it had been first things first, and all thought of dating had been put aside. But now it was time. Where should he go to begin? A friend suggested a church group for singles, and that seemed as good a place as any to meet new people.

You can imagine his surprise when he bumped into two old girlfriends from high school who were both single and looking too. He and one of them had dated for two years when they were both in high school. He asked her out and soon realized how much they both had matured over the years.

. . . .

I was right to wait because now I am comfortable and ready to date seriously.

Several times now Donald and Maria had
gone out, first to dinner, then to a ball game
and on a third date to a comedy club, where
they laughed until their sides nearly split.
Commenting on how much fun they had at
the comedy club, Don mentioned he was pretty funny himself. She was surprised, for
while he was pleasant, she had not seen any
signs of humor during any of their dates.

On their next date all that changed. They
went to a huge party at the fraternity he
belonged to. As a senior he wasn't very active, but he did love to go to their parties.
Well, she saw his humor that night — in
everything short of wearing a lamp shade
on his head. She was mortified at what he
thought was humor. He was drunk and
when he finally took the time to look for
Maria she was long gone, having taken a
cab home alone.

· · · · · · · ·

*I have pride in myself and don't need to
date a person who needs liquor to be funny.*

Hal had been in a wheelchair since he had an auto accident three years before. Even though he was a paraplegic — he was a vibrant, exciting and handsome man.

After a while he adjusted to being in the wheelchair and bought a special van which became his and his friends' main transportation. As long as a place was accessible, they were game to try it, which is why, one evening, they all found themselves at a play.

As usual, during the intermission Hal was surrounded by a group of people. "How do you do it, Hal? I'm really jealous. Maybe it's because you're in the chair."

Hal started to roar. "You always used to say that even before my accident? I just like people and strike up conversations with them. Most people want to talk, so I've learned to listen. That's my big secret!"

. . . .

People are drawn to those who pay attention and hear between the lines. I am blessed to be a good listener and I'm able to really hear.

Sheila and her boyfriend Lenny really got along famously. They had been dating for a long while and had settled into a routine — each evening they spent together with friends.

Later at home that evening, Lenny said, "Judy's new boyfriend reeks of cologne and talks non-stop. What did you think?"

"I like him; he seems like a nice enough guy. But what about Lucy's date, wasn't he weird?"

It didn't take too long to recognize that their criticisms were becoming malicious and hurtful. They finally agreed not to criticize each other's friends again. It worked better all around that way.

• • • • • • • •

Before I insert my large foot into my small mouth,
I had better give careful thought to what
malicious talk says about me.

When two people begin to date, naturally feelings for one another grow. Soon their affection and physical feelings for one another also increase. Beginning with gentle touching and kissing, many couples progress rather quickly to having sex.

This is not satisfactory for some who are not ready for a full sexual commitment yet and may be afraid of the diseases that run so rampant these days. They may ask their partners to refrain from intercourse for now.

Every person has their own feelings, and if the partner can respect this need and express love and caring in other ways, intercourse need not be a part of the relationship until much later.

· · · · · · · ·

Making love is not a prerequisite I must accept in order to date. I decide when and with whom I shall make love.

For some reason these days it seems that every time someone goes out with a new date, that person is evaluated in terms of whether they would make a good prospective steady or mate.

What happened to the days of dating just for the joy of dating, for the excitement of having a new friend with whom to do things? Too many people feel as if they are in a "meat market," waiting to be sold to the highest bidder.

Dating itself can be enough for many people who want a friend to see a movie with, who want a special person to take out to dinner or to join them at a party.

• • • • • • • •

Dating need not always be the means to an
end but can be the actual goal itself —
the goal of fun and companionship.

Her last child had moved out of the house. For the first time in three decades she was alone — completely alone. And she was loving it. Her new-found privacy and having to account for one felt delightful.

After so many years of always being responsible to someone, of having to share her car, of erratic meals and meals missed that she had spent long hours preparing, this seemed like heaven. For a few months.

Then her friends began to push her to get serious with a man she had been dating casually. "You don't want to be alone when you get old, do you?" Immediately defensive, she said it didn't matter, that she wasn't going to get serious just for fear of being alone.

· · · · · · · ·

Having waited so long for some modicum of privacy, I am not willing to give it up because someone told me to. I am a strong woman and can make my own decisions.

Harris had been born with one arm a bit shorter than the other. Naturally in elementary school he took some teasing, but as he matured he rarely thought about it any more unless he was buying a new suit and the tailor was shortening the sleeve.

This time, to his surprise, the tailor was a seamstress, newly hired by the store where he always bought his suits. She was pretty, with long red hair and sparkling green eyes, and her name was Kaitlinn. He enjoyed talking with her and was sorry when the fitting was over.

When he went to pick up the suit, he asked to see her and inquired, "Are you married or engaged?" She told him no and he promptly asked her out. She said yes. On the way home he was whistling and thankful, for the very first time, for his short arm.

. . . .

*What should always matter is not what
I look like but who I am underneath.*

Diana was excited. This was the evening she was to meet her fiance Franz's parents for the first time. "Now remember, honey, they will love you because they know I do, but they don't speak English well and tend to speak German in the house."

She could tell they approved, for they had smiled and hugged her when she arrived. Still, she was a bit uncomfortable with Franz as an interpreter.

She insisted on helping with the dinner dishes and said, "I know you don't speak English well and that is fine. But if I am to be your daughter-in-law, don't you think we should at least try?"

With damp eyes and a wide smile her future mother-in-law said, "You pretty. You nice. Franz love you." They hugged, and the seeds of a lovely relationship were planted.

· · · · · · · ·

Sometimes good intentions are not enough.
I need to show I care with positive action.

Virginia was feeling short-changed. Her boyfriend Will never did any of those little things so many other men do. No flowers. No little love presents.

"Why can't you be like Nancy's boyfriend, Dick? He always remembers her with little presents, cards and love notes. It's not the gifts I care about, but I sure do covet those little love notes!"

William was surprised. He had been thinking only the other day how much he loved Virginia, and he was soon going to ask her to marry him but her reaction frightened him off.

She realized how much he loved her and that their love need never come in the form of presents. Better measures of love are caring, sharing, hugging, holding and devotion.

. . . .

My strong sense of self allows me to feel
neither hurt nor worry, as we both
will move along at our own pace.

It didn't seem to matter what she did for her boyfriend, it was never enough. If she did his laundry, he would lament that she hadn't done his ironing as well. If she ironed, she would then be chastised for using too much or too little starch.

It definitely seemed a no-win situation, yet he was sweet and charming — just often enough to keep her hooked. Hurt and angry, she finally wrote him a note expressing her feelings.

He was shocked, for he had not realized at all what he was doing and how it must sound. Forgiven, with better understanding between one another, they remembered from then on to ask when they wanted specific favors, to praise each other and to always remember to say "thank you for your help."

· · · · · · · ·

It is amazing what the words thank you can bring to a relationship. I hope never to take my loved one for granted again.

How much fun we all had at the circus when we were young. From the acrobats to cotton candy, to clowns to the ringmaster, the circus became part of the fiber of our childhoods.

When a fun-loving yet mature person meets and falls in love with a mature but more somber adult, a real challenge is at hand. So long as the fun-loving person is appropriate and knows how to separate work and play, everything can be all right.

Some of the more somber people are really quite amenable to learning how to play. They just never had the opportunity as children. For one reason or another they now have the time and the willingness to play, and play they do. Those who can't or won't learn never will — poor souls.

• • • • • • • •

Saying good-bye to a person I love very much is hard, but if that person has not developed a fun-loving nature by now, they never will.

301

May and Ronnie met three years ago. It seemed that every party one attended found the other there, too. After months of coincidence and casual conversations, they finally decided to go out for a date. From that evening forward they became inseparable.

All their friends thought they would soon marry; so did May and her family. Ronnie was such a fine young man. One day they had a picnic in a local park. A youngster missed a ball which landed right in their potato salad. May stood up, threw both the ball and the potato salad right at him and cussed him up and down. Quickly apologetic to both the child and Ronnie, she tried to explain her behavior, but Ronnie understood that she had been concealing a bad temper and didn't like children. Time proved him right, and he backed out of their relationship.

. . . .

I have control over my temper and would not marry a person who can't discuss problems rationally.

October 29   *Call On Harley*

Three female roommates were planning another party. They couldn't even out the guys and gals, so they decided to call good old Harley. What they didn't know was that he had a mad crush on one of them. Harley was happy to be invited but he tended to fade into the woodwork. Still, it was a nice party and the food was good.

One day he sat down with Rae and told her the truth. "I've had a crush on you since the eighth grade. Could you ever consider getting serious with me?" Rae started to laugh at first, not sure he was really serious. When she saw he was, she said, "No way, buddy. You are just not my type." With that she turned and walked away, leaving him embarrassed and hurt.

· · · · · · · ·

*Being used is a rotten feeling. If I am being used,
I will look for a new group of friends —
friends who will appreciate me for who I am.*

"I'm never going to be like my father," Ross insisted "He never had anything to offer us but the back of his hand." His friendship with Alma was deepening with each date. One evening Ross asked Alma for her hand in marriage. She cried, hugging him and said yes.

As time passed three lovely chilcen came along. True to his word, Ross was a very good and involved parent, until one day. After Little League he stormed into Ross, Jr's. room and gave him a beating. "I can't believe you lost that tournament single-handedly," he screamed. "You stupid, worthless . . ."

Afraid for her son's life, Alma called the police, signed a formal complaint and had Ross removed from their home.

· · · · · · · ·

Protecting my loved ones also includes
the price I am willing to pay. I am
not frightened to bring criminal proceedings to save
my child and possibly my marriage.

Luann was so tired of it all. She would meet a nice man, and as soon as he found out she was a psychiatrist, he would stop dating her. The very word "psychiatry" put off many men.

"Don't tell anyone tonight what I do," whispered Luann to her closest friend, Andrea. "I'm going to play it safe tonight. I won't lie, but I won't volunteer any information either."

She wore jeans and little make-up and let people draw their own conclusions. Tonight men who might have never approached her before did, and she had a wonderful time.

• • • • • • • •

Although proud of my profession, I want who I am to attract potential dates, not what I do.

Leif and Ali had been married for 12 years. They worked hard, built a home, had two children and got a dog. When Ali lost her job, things started to change. "I'd like to stay home a while and be here for the children."

It was hard at first to be home after all those years of working, but soon she came to love it. Over the months her life settled into housework, shopping and doing light cooking for her family. It also included drinking beer. Leif recognized that besides a pre-dinner drink with him, she was downing at least a six-pack each day.

"Ali, we have to talk," said Leif nervously. "I think you're an alcoholic. You drink way too much, honey." She was furious with Leif, but eventually they talked about it. She finally agreed her problem was boredom and promised to go look for work. They agreed, for the time being, to wait and see.

• • • • • • • •

Everyone deserves a second chance, and since I love my partner I intend to offer that chance.

Lately it seems to be all the rage on radio and television talk shows. Infidelity. We are told to watch tomorrow for "Husbands who have affairs and still stay married to their wives!" or "Father makes love to his son's fiance!" Our world seems overly involved in the sordid details of other people's lives.

It's a whole different story when the infidelity is happening to us. Whether married or seriously dating, we are deeply hurt when we find out our loved one isn't being faithful to us. What should we do now?

Some people talk it over, stop the behavior and are truly able to forgive. Others try hard to set it aside, staying together and trying to ignore the problem. The largest group, however, leaves the relationship and gets on with their lives. This is very hard to do, but extremely wise.

• • • • • • • •

By remembering that a person who cheats on their partner will cheat again, I am glad I have the fortitude to leave.

The question has been asked since time immemorial. How much should I tell my boyfriend or girlfriend, husband or wife about my past? Should I tell about lovers I have had or that I gave up a baby for adoption when I was 14? Should I tell that I was once treated for a sexually transmitted disease?

Each person decides what is best for them and then must live with the decision. However, once the decision has been made, it must be final. If the truth is told, you must be prepared to accept the consequences of possibly losing the one you love. Additionally, we have to accept that if we tell the truth it might be used against us someday. So the problem is serious — weighing truth and trust against secrecy and possible exposure.

• • • • • • • •

Couples who are in love can keep each other's secrets. Once they give their word, resentment and anger must be put away and complete trust should take their place.

Each of us wants some measure of control in our lives. From where we live to what kind of car we drive, we exercise personal control without thinking much about it.

The situation changes when we begin to date a person who feels the need to control us. Denise learned this when she was told "We're going to an office party Saturday night to welcome our new district manager. Wear that low-cut black dress with the silver shoes. And be ready at 6:45."

She went along, smiled and looked lovely, but afterwards they had a long talk about his need to control her and her expectations that they would be sharing decisions.

By the end of the conversation, she knew he would not be able to change. She kissed him goodbye and walked away in tears.

· · · · · · · ·

I dislike being ordered around. I do not need to stay with a partner who tries to control my life.

309

For a long while they were casual friends, living in the same apartment complex and meeting at the pool, in the party room or at the home of mutual friends. Brian wanted more but Janine kept putting him off each time he called to ask her out.

Finally he convinced her to meet him at a hamburger joint nearby. "All right, Janine. I've known you for a long time. Why are you scared? I would never hurt you. Please share with me what is keeping you from dating."

And she did. About her breakdown ten years before and the three months in the psychiatric ward. She had been fine for all these years. "So?" he replied. "That's ancient history. Mental illness is nothing to be ashamed of. Now, will you please go out with me?" With the weight of the world lifted off her shoulders, she said "Yes!"

. . . .

*Mental illness, like physical illness, is part
of life and needn't be shamful anymore. I
need not hide in the shadows of my life.*

What a weird feeling to become part of that group of people who frequent singles bars and dances searching for the perfect potential person to date. Everyone, it seemed, had someone to dance with but Nina and Mollie, who were still sitting and waiting.

Mollie, who considered herself average looking at best, spotted an absolute Adonis two tables over. She elbowed Nina. "Look at him! He is by far the most gorgeous hunk I have ever laid eyes on. There's no way a guy like him will ever notice me."

"Go for the brass ring, Mollie, just this once. The worst thing that can happen is that he will say no." With lead feet Mollie went over and asked him to dance. He flashed her a wonderful smile and said, "Well, sure!" That wonderful smile was the same one he flashed at her thousands of times in their subsequent and very happy marriage.

. . . .

Opportunities for the brass ring come rarely in life. I will go for them when they do come along.

It seemed as though they were a perfect couple, well suited with similar educations and interests. It appeared that they would be happy.

She usually planned their dates but every now and then he would contribute. Yet before too long he had fewer ideas and didn't like the ones she came up with each week.

One evening she sat him down and said, "Our time together is boring. Can't we do something different or spontaneous once in a while? We used to have so much fun together. He was upset at her attitude and let her stalk out of the restaurant. Sadly he let her go knowing the fault was his but unwilling to change.

. . . .

Grieving lost love won't help me.
I need to learn to share, to plan together and
then to move on with my life.

She didn't know what to do. She was married to the most wonderful man. However, he had virtually no sex drive. She tried talking with him, dressing up in a sexually stimulating clothes and even meeting him one evening nude at the door.

His body reacted normally, but she could always tell any affection she ever got was faked and that he had virtually no interest in sex. He was not gay, for they talked frankly about it and there was really no indication that he was. So they were at an impasse.

Finally she decided she would allow herself a "gentleman out-call escort." She was most cautious with all the problems with AIDS and other sexually transmitted diseases, but she discovered enjoyable sex she never had found at home. She told no one, but her attitude about her marriage, which was really quite strong in other areas, improved vastly.

• • • • • • • •

I make the choices I feel are right for me, even if I may have to keep them secret.

313

Who among us doesn't remember that day in grade school when the boys and girls were separated and we were subjected to a lecture or film about the facts of life? As kids we were always too embarrassed to ask a single question.

Ken and Mandy were talking about it one day after they had been dating seriously for a while. Neither remembered how they got on that particular topic, but both were laughing as they talked. Ken had known for months that Mandy was a virgin, but he was pleased about it. She wanted to save herself for her one true love.

As they walked down the aisle, loving friends and family smiled at how well-suited they were to each other and how happy they were going to be together.

· · · · · · · ·

A personal code of ethics means different things to each of us. I respect and appreciate my partner's values.

She awakened to hear the birds calling to one another and to see the sun rising. "Tim," she said, after he picked up the phone, "Get up quickly and look at the sunrise!"

"Oh, I did," he answered. "It was just gorgeous!"

Within a few days their furnishings would be together and so would they — but not until after the cruise where they were to be married. They had invited all five of their children, the children's spouses and the grandchildren to come along for the wedding.

New love for these older people — this time happening in Leisure World — gave both of them a sense of renewed youth. The joy that each felt when seeing the other was greater than at any other time of their lives.

• • • • • • • •

Regardless of how old we are, being in love puts spring into our steps, purpose into our lives and excitement for every day yet to be shared.

Len and his twin brother Gary were the only two children of older parents. Their father was retired by the time the boys were finished with high school so life was very simple and routine at their house. Their lives were rather quiet.

When Gary met Tara, he saw the other side of life. Her young family didn't always eat together but when they did it was fun and enjoyable each time. He appreciated their healthy meals, especially Tara's home-made bread. Gary loved Tara already by then but years later he would still grin when he told anyone, "It was the homemade bread that made me fall for her!" The same skill and patience she used when baking bread was shown to him during all the years of their life together.

· · · · · · · ·

I will work hard to maintain a healthy balance in my marriage.

It was an unusual circumstance. Having met at a clambake in their early 20s, Abby and Ira were definitely in love. Her family loved him, and their families enjoyed being with each other.

Then one day Abby's old boyfriend re-entered the picture, and her feelings for him were still so strong that she broke it off with Ira. Both he and their families were shattered. Abby's sister, Dianne, called him to say how sorry she was and they wound up going out. Ira liked her, and before long they were in love.

To everyone's surprise they eloped after a three-month courtship. After the initial discomfort of being around Abby dissipated, Dianne and Abby stayed close and Ira had a wonderful, warm and loving wife.

· · · · · · · ·

By keeping our eyes open, we don't miss
a chance which could have easily been overlooked.

Anyone who has had the joy of watching mourning doves doing their mating dance or who has watched swans dance when mating knows it's a fantastic sight one never forgets. The beautiful and exquisite rituals are repeated at the same time each year.

Now we are doing a whole different mating dance. Single again, we are now ready to meet someone new, someone special.

Doing the mating dance and then actually winning that person's love means we have finally learned enough about ourselves and our needs to seek out the right mate. Ready to mate for life, we are totally enamored with our newfound love and are truly committed to a life spent together.

• • • • • • • •

As we take part in the mating dance,
we become excited when we realize what
wonderful things life holds in store for us.

In the first five years she had been a teacher, never once had a student said "Yes, Ma'am" to her. Now that she had been hired as an overseas teacher for the dependents of servicemen, she was hearing "Yes, Ma'am" constantly. One evening Private Claridge came in for a conference about his daughter. "Please sit down, Mr. Claridge. Thank you for coming."

"Yes, Ma'am," he answered shyly. His wife had died the year before so he tried hard to help Jenny with her schoolwork. "She misses her mother so much — and so do I — that we still both have trouble concentrating."

She let him talk and then cry about his love for his wife and what a gap her death had left. She offered to tutor Jenny and two years later she was the second Mrs. Claridge.

· · · · · · · ·

Life makes offers to us all the time;
we just need to decide to accept them.

Jake enjoyed his job as an auto mechanic and was very good at his work. Constant raises and excellent job reviews indicated that he was one of the best. One morning Ms. Wolf, a lawyer, brought in her sports car to be fixed. A week later she called and asked to talk to him. Knowing he was single she invited him for a homemade meal to repay him for finally fixing her car.

He accepted and they both had a nice evening. A few days later she called and invited him to a play she had tickets for. Jake couldn't believe a lady with such a good education would be interested in him, but he went and they had a great time. He then asked her out and she accepted, and they began a new relationship.

• • • • • • • •

My job is no indication of who I am underneath.
I am proud that I do my job well and
that I met a very special person because of my work.

Boris emigrated from Russia to the United States. He worked hard to learn English and got a job as an engineer. He met a co-worker, Angela, who was black. He thought she was nice and they became close friends. Soon they began to date and then fell in love. They dated for a long while; they understood interracial marriage is still frowned upon by many people.

After three years they decided to marry. As he adjusted his tie on his tuxedo shirt, he smiled at his reflection. He thought, only in America would I have the opportunity to marry the woman I love. I am so happy to be an American.

Boris and his wife loved each other truly. Over the years they never stopped loving each other or working on their marriage.

• • • • • • • •

Marriage is a contract which takes thoughtful and constant negotiation. I will always try to to show and honor my love.

Hurrying was built into his lifestyle. Taxis and subways, shoulder to shoulder with other people scurrying about on the sidewalk — all this is New York. And all of this Nick adored. As a rising star in his business Nick hadn't had much time to date, but word was filtering down from top management that he really needed to be married to get any higher up the corporate ladder.

When he met Barb at a party he looked at her with new eyes, realized he was ready to settle down and asked her out. They got on well together and ultimately fell in love. The only problem was that she was a Californian and owned her own business there.

Later, Nick left his job willingly to move to California and get married. A year earlier nothing had mattered but work — funny how feelings change.

· · · · · · · ·

Keeping an open mind helps guarantee I will not miss a golden opportunity when it arrives.

Aspiring to goals and working hard to reach them is what most of us were taught. So many of us remember being told, "You can be anything you want to be if you work hard enough." A problem may arise when two fall for each other when their goals and aspirations are totally disparate.

Wendy was in college working hard to get a degree in international business. Alan, her boyfriend, still lived with his family.

Alan knew deep in his heart that it wouldn't last and that she would eventually fall in love with someone with an education and higher goals. The truth was she loved him and wanted him to move with her, but he just knew their union wasn't meant to be.

· · · · · · · ·

Even though I have my own job, I would never want to feel "kept." In order to preserve my dignity I choose to leave.

It was a wonderful and often romantic courtship. Since Courtney had been so hurt by her former boyfriend, she had been especially cautious before letting herself fall in love with Danny.

They each dated the other, always on the lookout for creative, fun and relatively inexpensive ways to date, with only an occasional rare splurge. What a joy it was for the two of them after their wedding — months later and then years later they were still best friends and lovers.

Those who know the true joy of being both best friends and lovers — and still know how to work at marriage and stay committed after years — are among the rare and fortunate few.

· · · · · · · ·

Commitment is the key word. By putting each other's needs first and always working on our marriage, we have kept its freshness and unique qualities alive.

We can't hide from the fact that affairs do happen during marriage. Winston had affairs constantly, one after another, mostly for sex and rarely for intellectual stimulation.

Ingrid knew about them all, but she figured since he kept coming home to her, since he was in her bed most nights and since they were, in their own way, devoted, she would look past all his affairs as though nothing had happened at all.

One morning she awakened ill. Her doctors asked if she was promiscuous. "Never! But my husband is."

"He has put you at great risk of contracting AIDS. You are HIV positive."

Ingrid was furious. "Over and over you put me at risk. Now my life is threatened! Get out and stay out!"

· · · · · · · ·

None of us today can take a chance
with our sexual behavior. We must
take care to always be protected.

It was a secret they had shared for a long time. Her husband treated her well except when they were being intimate. Then he became aggressive and even abusive. He would hug her too hard — until her ribs hurt and she would beg for mercy.

She had thoroughly enjoyed sex with other men before she met her husband, but from the very first time they had sex she never enjoyed it again. She rationalized that each person makes love differently and that this was his way.

One evening she went to a meeting about abuse, coaxed by a girlfriend who needed someone to go with her. As the meeting unfolded she suddenly realized that for 12 years she had been a victim of abuse — sexual abuse. He was overpowering her during sex to fulfill his needs.

· · · · · · · ·

Getting out of an abusive situation is paramount to me but I need help. I would like us to get help together but I don't know how.

326

It is said that the single biggest item couples fight about is money. Most of us can relate to this topic closely. Money — we never have enough. And when we do get it, we may disagree about how to spend it.

Some folks have been raised in a "cash only" mode — if you don't have cash, you don't buy it. Others use credit cards to the limit and spend their lives juggling payments. They spend more time figuring out their payment schedules than they did shopping.

Two people who have fallen in love need to discuss money and how they will handle it, who will pay bills and how much they will save — before they commit to spending their lives together. Doing so in advance will offer both a good understanding of the other's habits and will potentially lower the risk in new marriages.

• • • • • • • •

By discussing money problems ahead of time, we reduce the risk of potentially damaging our relationship.

Cindy had given up a child for adoption when she was 15. There wasn't a day that she didn't think of her son. It was a secret no one but her doctors and the social worker knew.

When Cindy met Sam and they got serious, she didn't tell him, even after their marriage. One day Sam remarked, "Honey, every November 23 you get so pensive and sad. Why?"

Drawing a deep breath she told him, thinking for sure her marriage was over. "Oh, honey, what a brave person you are. To make such a mature decision at such a young age. I'm so proud of you." From that time forward every November 23 one red rose arrived. "I love you," the note said, "and I always will."

• • • • • • • •

*Sometimes a secret that seems too terrible
to mention loses its potency when it
is shared with someone we love.*

Herb and Trina were at the state fair with their children, each having a great time. "Corn dogs first, please, Daddy!" shrieked their three-year-old.

"Nope. Milkshakes first this time, remember?" But first they all went to the midway where Ricky won a huge stuffed dog, then they sought out everyone's favorite food. That way the parents would be able to enjoy the craft show. Finally, in the animal petting area, the tired family sat down to rest.

"Honey! Look over there at the fat bald guy near the baby lambs. He used to be my high school beau. I went steady with him for nearly three years. Boy, you talk about love being frozen in time!"

• • • • • • • •

We can never go back to the way we were,
but we can move on to more personally enriching
relationships in the future.

It had been a long courtship but appeared worth it all. Faye and Geoff, both in their late 70s, were going to tie the knot. This union was a combination of the very wonderful and the very hard. For two years their marriage was made in heaven.

Then, in a stormy turn of events, Faye's only daughter and her husband were killed. Their three small children were left unscathed by the murderer.

When the will was read, the children were to be raised by their Grandma Faye. Thank goodness the children had Faye. But they did not have her husband Geoff. He had a fit. "I have already put in my time and money for children and have no intention of doing it again." Faye tried to pacify him, but it was obvious the children must come first. The man she thought she would love forever left her life completely.

. . . .

I am now strong enough to choose
a path I never thought I'd have to follow.

Of course we have all heard the phrase, "Love is blind." We see beauty where someone else would see a plain person. We see perfection when another person might view that same individual as flawed.

Love can cause us to look past any shortcomings our loved one may actually have. While most of us do eventually notice, by then true love has entered into the equation and we love the person unconditionally.

She doesn't see that he is going bald, only that he gives her an adoring smile. Even though she might be ten pounds too heavy, his heart still jumps when she enters the room. This is part of the wonderful joy of being in love.

. . . .

One of life's wonders is that love is blind.
Soon I hope to find the person who
makes my heart jump with joy.

Earl and Trudi were as much in love with each other as everyone else is in the beginning. They really wanted an equal relationship, equal housecleaning and equal help in parenting once they had children.

Earl was slowly having more problems with drinking. Trudi continued to be a strong student and a good mother. Her family helped when possible, and without even realizing it, Earl was completely squeezed out.

It wasn't easy but she persevered. Trudi got her degree by the time her youngest was in first grade. She continued on her self-improvement program. They were still married, and Earl was not changing or growing at all. Soon she asked him for a divorce, accepted a job across the country, took the children and left.

. . . .

*My desire to be better myself has taken
fortitude but I respect myself and
intend to reach my goals.*

George could recall times during childhood when he felt sad for long periods of time. When he was ready to move out on his own he was both elated and frightened. Once a year or so he would become very depressed.

Finally he saw a psychologist who treated his depression as needed. George recovered very well.

One day at a friend's party he met Sandi, the nicest person he had ever met. Their dating soon became serious and they began to talk about getting married. George was scared but wanted her to know the truth. "Darling, I want you to know that I have always had to deal with mild bouts of depression." She assured him they would do fine. For one thing depression was an illness — one that her father had dealt with so she was no stranger to it. George was so relieved.

• • • • • • • •

A tendency to feel depressed is no reason to back off from life — if I did, look what I would be missing.

She loved to sing and had a double major in voice and piano. One day at the student union she met a guy who she had heard was quite a good musician himself. "Neat," she commented. "Maybe we can get together sometime?"

Adam agreed it might be fun to go out with Elizabeth, and they met on Tuesday for dinner. Unfortunately they found they were not a good match. She was very much a blue jean and flannel shirt sort while he was into three piece suits all the way. Still, they did eat dinner and stay to talk a while.

What a surprise — they actually turned out to like each other. Over the weeks they became very close. Instead of opera she began to sing some jazz, and instead of pop he softened a bit to classical and country. They formed a duo and took the country by storm. They soon got engaged and married.

· · · · · · · ·

Willingness to take a chance shows strong moral fortitude and a great deal of curiosity.

Every few months Corky had a brand new boyfriend. She often brought home new male friends. Needless to say her family were concerned. "I just haven't found the right man yet. Believe me, you'll be the first to know when I do."

One spring vacation she met a lovely young man in Florida. No vacation could have been more wonderful. Corky and Max eloped on their last night in Sarasota, a plan they agreed on to prevent a big wedding neither wanted.

Wiring ahead that Mr. and Mrs. Max Winston III were arriving Saturday night gave her family a tremendous kick. Her confused parents opened the door to be greeted by a wonderful new son-in-law. They adored him too.

• • • • • • • •

Just because I had a number of false starts doesn't mean I'm no longer in the race.

It seemed appropriate. On a dismal winter day, Ellen and Bernie ended their long relationship. He broke up with her one night at dinner. For almost two hours she couldn't leave the restaurant, but sat there with her chin nearly hanging in her soup.

Ellen had been totally in love with Bernie but it was over so fast that she never got the opportunity to tell him so or even say goodbye. She regretted how it ended for a long while. "If only we had talked about it first," she thought, even though she knew it would have made no difference in the end.

Every person needs and wants to be loved, and for every love that breaks up there is always someone left bleeding — deep inside where no one else can see. When that happens, feelings of unworthiness and of being unlovable return.

. . . .

*Breaking up is hard but I have made
the decision to end this unhealthy relationship
and move on with my life.*

It's not an uncommon scenario. During business hours a man or woman is courteous to colleagues and well-liked by everyone at work. When that person arrives home, it seems as if they have used up their daily quotient of patience and have nothing left for their loved ones.

Turning on the television, hiding behind a newspaper, doing work brought home from the office or blatantly ignoring their spouse are all indications that respect for one another has disappeared.

Mutual respect can be reinstated in a marriage with desire on the part of both parties and willingness to seek help. If the marriage is salvageable, then the two need to remember why they fell in love in the first place, how they used to feel and then work hard to regain those feelings.

· · · · · · · ·

I respect myself enough
to know that I will never treat
my love with disrespect.

337

Some people have such perfect manners that they can hardly tolerate anyone who does not. This was the case with Lizzie and Karl. Lizzie was willing to go to a charming Italian restaurant with Karl when he first asked her out. She was so appalled by his table manners she would never go out with him again. After calling her and getting nowhere he appeared at her door one evening. She graciously invited him in. "Why have you not answered my many calls?" he asked sadly.

Lizzie really listened to what he had to say that evening. She discovered he was in a new country and wanted very much to look right, to act right, to dress well and to be accepted. "All right," she finally agreed, "I'll tutor you — but nothing else, okay?" For months she did, and then they had a splendid graduation dinner.

· · · · · · · ·

I may be surprised at
the gem someone may be under a
seemingly rough exterior.

When Brenda won two tickets to Disney World, she couldn't believe her luck. She could either ask her roommate, her mother or Ian, a man she had dated for about a month and liked very well. She decided to ask Ian. After all, what better way to really learn about a person than to spend a ten-day vacation together?

Brenda was in for the surprise of her life. Ian turned out to be a joy to be with all the time. He was agreeable, funny, serious, a wonderful lover, spontaneous and in love with Brenda. They talked all the time — about serious goals, mundane topics, a comic in the daily paper. It was as if they had been best friends for life.

· · · · · · · ·

Unless I take a risk, I may never
make any discoveries. What a joy to have made
this discovery of a life-mate to love.

| December 5 | *Balloons Or Flowers?* |

It was a real "Dating Game" match. She chose Dave, a construction worker who had never been married. His video reflected a good sense of humor.

She was nervous before her date, but then he arrived with one red rose, a balloon and a box of candy. He couldn't have gone wrong.

He had a great sense of humor and he was handsome. But one thing was very wrong. All he wanted to talk about was himself. At first she thought he was out to impress her, but before long she realized that he really didn't know how to carry on a decent conversation.

She couldn't wait to get home. Unfortunately for Marlene and Dave there was to be no love connection.

• • • • • • • •

I accept the fact that sometimes relationships don't work out, but as long as I feel good about myself, I know eventually someone wonderful will enter my life.

Remember hearing, "What do you guys think I am? Made of money?" As children we had no concept of budgeting; it had to be carefully taught to us with many other lessons we learned as children.

So we grew up enough to get a part-time job and found it was hard to make money and even harder to save any of it. Later we got a full-time job, fell in love and started saving for a ring or a wedding. Then along came children and more bills than we had money to cover.

In a matter of moments it seems, we went from hearing, "What do you guys think I am? Made of money?" to saying those very words to our own children. They will grow up in due time just as we did.

• • • • • • • •

I realize now that everything in life changes, but the best part is that so much of it stays the same.

Most of us have been raised with a strong work ethic. In fact, when we were children, our parents continually reminded us that "The world doesn't owe anyone a living," along with dozens of other "parentisms."

Funny, but as we get older the comments we never understood as children all make perfect sense now. "Laugh and the world laughs with you. Cry and you cry alone." and "He who gives, gets." We called them "words our parents taught us to live by," and they surely make sense now.

One phrase, however, doesn't always work. "Give that person just one more chance." Try as we might, that one person who seemed so right for the first several dates turned out to have a hidden personality problem or was just plain boring. While we really did try, parents aren't always right.

· · · · · · · ·

I certainly trust and believe
my parents, but I am an adult now and can
make my own decisions.

After weeks of sitting in booths near each other and eating dinner separately, Lou asked Zena if she would like to have dinner with him. They were very much alike. So they began to date. It didn't take long before they were in a serious relationship.

That is, it was serious until the night Lou told her he had a couple of joints and asked if she would like to smoke some pot with him. Actually, the more she thought about it, he liked to drink an awful lot of beer as well.

She could handle a bit of drinking but was genuinely concerned that he either had or was developing a drug problem. On the basis of that information and her fear about the drug use, she left both Lou and the coffee shop.

. . . .

*Only time helps us know
another person intimately. If we don't
like what we see, then we can move
on as I have chosen to do.*

Men and women are different; men have few close friends or rarely talk about feelings or significant events in their lives and tend to keep feelings bottled up. So we are told.

Janet did not believe those things because Marty was not only warm and wonderful but he talked to her about everything, was interested in her goals and aspirations and she had even seen him cry in a movie theater. Today he had told her he loved her in front of their friends at a restaurant.

Janet was ready to get married, yet somehow, deep down, she had the sense that not all Marty was saying rang true. He was warm and gave great back rubs. But she later broke off their engagement because he was too insecure about her career.

· · · · · · · ·

*When words and deeds don't match
and when apprehension creeps in, it is time
to rethink the relationship.*

In many households children were de-lighted when they were told, "I'll do that for you. You go out and have some fun." Other parents expected their kids to do almost all the chores and even work a part-time job.

Neither of these types of families were preparing their children for what would happen in real life, when they moved out on their own.

Today the wise person pays careful atten-tion to note if someone they are dating is messy or neat or if their apartment is clean or messy. All successful marriages find their own equilibrium and ways to share that are acceptable to each person.

. . . .

In order to have a balanced marriage,
both people must be grounded in their basic
life skills. I feel very grounded.

One evening at a party one person suggested they write down the best things that
had ever happened to them as children.
What a variety — from getting their first
puppy to the lead in a class play — the lists
were interesting.

All except Perry's, which was blank. He
just listened. Later his fiancee asked why he
hadn't joined in. His answer surprised her,
"My childhood was awful; my dad died when
I was seven so I became the 'little man,' doing what I could to help my mom.

"Then one evening when I was 11, Mom
climbed into bed with me and touched me. I
was terrified. When I was 15, I packed up
and left. I know she probably did it to my
brothers too, but I had to leave to save myself. I'm hurt and embarrassed that I never
told you, but now I know that it's time for
me to get some professional help."

• • • • • • • •

I promise to support my partner
and to express my love and care every day.

346

No one likes to apologize. We remember as children when our parents insisted we apologize to each other. We did, but as soon as their backs were turned we made faces again.

As adults it may not be so easy to apologize, especially if we know we have deeply hurt someone's feelings. Mustering inner strength to apologize is hard but it must be done in order for all people involved to feel better and forgive one another.

Sometimes we wait too long to say, "I'm sorry," and then we lose the very people who matter to us most. Family feuds go on for years, the reason for their original split long forgotten, yet each family member clings to anger for no reason at all.

. . . .

Apologizing in time to those
we love with warmth and meaning not only
saves the relationship, it saves our
good feelings about ourselves.

Throughout life we encounter those who are terribly stubborn and those who are not. Learning the best way to deal with each personality type is not easy, but the sooner we learn the better our relationship is bound to become.

The less secure person particularly may have an awful time asking for help. From, "Hand me that screwdriver, please," to "Can we have stew for dinner?" to "Would you like to make love?" are questions that some people have to frame and reframe so it doesn't feel to them as if they are begging. Asking, "If it's not too much trouble and you are getting up, could you please bring me some water?" Their insecurity is so apparent that it hurts to watch.

• • • • • • • •

The secure person knows when
and how to ask for help. I am proud of my
ability to take care of my own needs.

348

My, how the two of them acted together. Just like colts in a field, playful, happy and full of joy.

Three years later, their thoughts turned to marriage. They anticipated a wonderful life together, a few children and years of happiness. As the date drew near, she wondered when she would get her engagement ring. Still, she loved him, and if the part about the ring was omitted, that would be fine. So they were married.

Five years later they went out for dinner for their anniversary. Perched on top of an anniversary cake was a diamond ring. "I can't believe it!"

"Well," he explained, "I didn't have any money when we got engaged, and now that I do, it's time for you to have what you should have had five years ago."

. . . .

*Waiting often brings more results
than prodding. With a love as strong as ours,
a ring is not what matters most.*

Josh had heard for days, "Don't ask Helene out. She's as frigid as they come; ask anyone." But Josh thought she was beautiful and asked her out anyway. To his surprise, she was delighted with his invitation.

There was a basic difference between Josh and his friends. Josh was raised in a religious, old-fashioned family — one where he was taught never to believe in rumors. It never occurred to him to "make a move" on her in the first of several dates. When he did, he asked first if he might kiss her.

As they gently kissed, Josh got curious. "Why did you turn down everyone else's offer of a kiss but let me?"

"Easy," she replied. "No one respected me enough to wait or even to ask. You are very special, Josh."

· · · · · · · ·

Sometimes the slow and careful
approach is the only one that works. I will
treat all my dates with the same respect
I give to anyone else.

George was 67 and getting ready to go out with Effie, the love of his life, with all the excitement of a 15-year-old on his first date. His eye had been on her for five years, since her husband became ill with heart disease and died. Since George had known Roger fairly well, he felt uncomfortable in the beginning about wanting to go out with his widow. The conflict was there, but so was a great deal of hope. Now enough time had passed to ease the conflict, and he was going out with Effie. He had hoped that the two of them would be able to get along as more than just old friends.

Unbeknownst to him, Effie was fluttering about in front of her dressing table, acting like a teenager once again. When he picked her up, they grinned at each other. Slowly and carefully their love grew.

· · · · · · · ·

Hope can replace conflict as
an opportunity to begin life afresh,
with a loving and caring partner.

Most people remember when as children we couldn't wait for either Christmas or Hanukkah. With childish eagerness we looked at the special day as a day for presents, not for the religious aspect.

The calendar became so much a part of our lives during our growing-up years. From family appointments to birthdays to baby-sitting jobs, the calendar ruled our lives.

As adults we now write what we wish to remember on the calendar. Our calendars are covered with business meetings, parties and especially dates with new people we are excited to spend time with. Rather than looking at it through a child's eyes, we now have our eyes on our own special times.

· · · · · · · ·

Marking calendars is our way of recording life's joys and tragedies. Nowadays they have become an exciting way of keeping track of our new social life.

"The one with the blond curly hair? See her?" whispered Don to Abdul. "She would never go out with me. She's the kind of girl reserved for the football team." So he never asked her out.

Life went on, and they both married different people. Two decades had passed when Don, who was divorced, heard her husband had died. He sat down and wrote her a card, saying how very sorry he was. To Don's surprise, she answered.

They began to write and make frequent phone calls. They finally got together and soon got married. "I can't believe you wanted to ask me out in high school! I was dying to go out with you. I waited and hoped, but you never asked."

• • • • • • • •

When opportunity is missed once
and another chance is offered, one should grab it.
Life may change when one takes a chance.

Lynn and Robert began their relationship during the winter hoping it would bloom to full love when spring arrived.

They went through all the dating rituals, from spending time in each other's apartments until eventually deciding it was time for dinner at each of their parents' homes. Robert's family was warm and charming. They all included Lynn in the conversation and let her know they approved of her.

It couldn't have been more different at her home. Lynn's parents were cool to Robert to the point of being rude. "Mama," she whispered in the kitchen, "don't you like him? What's wrong?"

"Well, of course we do, dear. We would have found a way to let you know if we didn't approve." Relaxed but perplexed, Lynn went back into the living room and sat down with Rob.

· · · · · · · ·

Our love is strong enough to handle
what appears to be rejection.

It was a strange quirk. He just loved horror films but they literally terrified his girlfriend. He did drag her to a few at first but decided that was silly. He tried to give them up but that didn't make a great deal of sense either.

He did not want to give up either his wonderful girlfriend or his lifelong collection of films, so they sat down to talk about it. They had to work hard for the compromise but they found a solution.

He didn't want to leave her at home and she didn't want to go, so they decided he would watch a movie in the living room and she would go to the bedroom or sun porch to read or visit with friends. That way they would be together yet apart and each could do what they liked best. Both were happy because they had worked hard to solve their problem.

. . . .

By keeping solutions simple and our minds open, we find that talking together solves our problems.

No two people who date do things in the same way. From all socioeconomic levels, from all walks of life, dating and courtship are treated differently.

Saul and Eva had dated for one month — every single night and every single day of the month. Eva invited Saul over to her place one Sunday and surprised him with champagne and cake. "Is this a special celebration or something?" he asked.

"Oh, Saul, don't you know? We've been together one whole incredible month. I've never had such a good time in my life." He hadn't realized it had been exactly one month, but he was delighted that she had.

From that time forward on the 21st of every month they share a kiss and champagne. For 36 years now they have been celebrating this special anniversary.

• • • • • • • •

Remembering small occasions
adds to the joy of being in love.

They met in the park on a beautiful Sunday afternoon. She was rollerblading and he was sort of rollerblading and being pulled by his dog. She petted the dog briefly and, as they skated around the lake and talked, they found they were neighbors.

As they skated over the weeks and dated over the months, his dog became less and less friendly. It became apparent that the dog saw her as a threat to his master. But by now he loved her and he loved his dog. Now what?

It was obvious a decision had to be made. To get rid of the dog seemed impossible. Now the dog growled each time she came close. He was obviously not the type of man who would place an animal before a person. The dog left. The lady became his wife.

. . . .

*My decision is made to put my
partner first in my life.*

All of us grew up with special family rituals. From special bedtime stories to family
birthday celebrations, we remember them
fondly.

Chester loved his family breakfast on
Christmas morning — breakfast first, presents after. Lisa's favorite was the first evening of Hanukkah when her family served
hot potato pancakes with applesauce and
they each opened one of their eight presents.

Chester and Lisa fell in love and were now
faced with the religion question. Either one
person had to give up their traditions and
religion and convert, or they could both attend both, with each maintaining their own
beliefs. They decided to marry and form
their own new combined family traditions
along with going to their parents' homes.

• • • • • • • •

Family traditions add so much to religion.
How I feel comes from deep within my soul and
it is always best when shared.

She had reluctantly accepted a casual date for Christmas Eve, since the invitation was to a play she was dying to see. Her date never showed up. Disappointed, wondering what she had done wrong she went to bed.

Next afternoon, propped at her back door was her date, complete with two crutches, one arm splint and a lopsided grin. He told her about his Laurel and Hardy attempt to get to her the night before.

Over supper they laughed and laughed. After all, one first had to picture his jacket, with the tickets in his pocket, in the front seat of his burning car. He had taken a life-saving leap from the car as soon as he realized it was on fire. So they first became close friends and were soon an item.

• • • • • • • •

Jumping to conclusions. If something in my life goes wrong I will try not to blame myself, there are many things in life that happen which I can't control

For those who celebrate Christmas and those who don't, the day can be glory-filled without religious connotations at all. Awakening in the morning and spending a few moments in bed assessing our lives — where we have been and where we are going is a wonderful way to start the day.

Birds singing or the glorious sight of trees covered with snow can fill anyone's day with glory. This is the day we can reach out to others who need our help — helping on a food line or doing a special favor for an elderly friend. This is a day for looking for joy, not for counting sadness.

. . . .

This is not a day to worry about
dating or looking for prospective mates.
Instead this is a day to reflect upon the meaning
of our lives and how we might choose to
enhance what we already enjoy.

At 32 it seemed her chances of ever loving again were getting slimmer with each year. She was sick. Not lovesick, just plain sick. Her multiple sclerosis was slight and only left her with a small limp.

Somehow it felt honorable to her that each time she went out she would announce to her date, "I have multiple sclerosis, you know," which would usually send him running for the nearest exit. Everytime she told she lost a potential suitor.

A good friend gave her some invaluable advice. "Don't tell about your MS until you are interested in him and know he is interested in you as well. If the feeling is mutual, then you should tell. Use common sense and do tell, but never dwell on the truth. After all, you have had MS for years and are living a wonderful life."

• • • • • • • •

Telling the whole truth too fast
pushes people away. I think enough of myself
to let them first get closer.

Loaded with books so high she couldn't see over them, Hope collided with a man who also couldn't see where he was going. Apologizing and picking up each other's belongings, they nearly collapsed laughing in the bookstore doorway.

That night Hope found his wallet in her knapsack. She called him to let him know she had it and he insisted on taking her to dinner. Her heart jumped with joy, as she was praying they would see each other again. A chance meeting caused an almost instant friendship. He was a senior in molecular biology and she a sophomore in biology. It didn't take too many months before their books were stacked together in their shared apartment.

• • • • • • • •

While we can't plan on chance
meetings, we can make the best of
them if they do occur.

Many people who used to share the holidays with families or friends are now alone. This makes holidays difficult to bear.

Who knows? If you were to go to a community-sponsored dinner or even invite people on your block who are also alone to dinner, you might start a whole new tradition. This was the case with Millie and Art. He came knocking on her door in their retirement community one morning and said he was alone for the holidays and was getting a group together to eat. Would she like to join them?

Overjoyed, she answered she would, at which point Art said, "Great! Now then, do you want to be turkey or pie?" She baked pies. Today she is still baking them for her husband Art.

. . . .

We should never be afraid to help those in need, all we have to do it try.

House cats. Of all things, it was his house cats that helped him decide. They had been dating casually, and he invited her over for Cantonese food he was going to cook himself.

"Be careful, my cats have hated every woman I've ever brought home." They walked in and the cats, two exquisite Siamese, immediately came to the door, rolled over and begged to be petted. "I must be in the wrong house," he said, with the oddest look on his face. "I have never seen them do this even with me."

"Oh, animals have always loved me because they can sense I love them." So the four of them had a lovely meal and he began to look at her with brand new eyes. After all, most people believe that animals are rarely wrong about people.

• • • • • • • •

The oddest reasons can bring people together,
I am grateful for the opportunities I have had.

Everyone has an ideal mate in mind — an ideal which changes when we meet a special new person who doesn't exactly fit our ideal.

It's a surprise how willing we are, like a willow tree bending in the wind, to bend toward a special person when the right wind blows. Those of us who want to find another person to love begin an active search. We ask friends if they know anyone for fix-ups, we look with open eyes to those people we see in our everyday lives.

And find them we do, for being loved, being cared about and sharing our lives matters so dearly.

. . . .

No one is perfect, so we learn to compromise our goals to complement each other.

Another year gone by — a year which may have been filled with disappointments or joy. We each have a brand new year coming up, a chance for countless new opportunities.

The last day of the year has arrived. In the morning when we awaken, we should be open and ready for whatever our world has to offer. This may be *the* year, the very best year for us — when our dreams, prayers and desires may be fulfilled.

Never giving up hope is one of the keys. We need to remember that in order to achieve our goals we must be in the right place. One never gets a job without applying; one never meets anyone new by staying at home.

· · · · · · · ·

Asking is the key — for a job, a date or help when we need it. May this year grant us all our dearest wishes.